The Critical Idiom

General Editor: JOHN D. JUMP

---

31   *Myth*

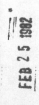

In the same series

Myth/ *K. K. Ruthven*

Methuen & Co Ltd

First published 1976
by Methuen & Co Ltd
11 New Fetter Lane London EC4P 4EE

© 1976 K. K. Ruthven

Filmset by Computer Photoset Ltd.
and printed in Great Britain by
Cambridge University Press

ISBN 0 416 78990 0 Hardback
ISBN 0 416 79000 3 Paperback

Distributed in the USA by
HARPER & ROW, PUBLISHERS INC
BARNES & NOBLE IMPORT DIVISION

To Simon, Guy and Patrick

Contents

General Editor's Preface

The volumes composing the Critical Idiom deal with a wide variety of key terms in our critical vocabulary. The purpose of the series differs from that served by the standard glossaries of literary terms. Many terms are adequately defined for the needs of students by the brief entries in these glossaries, and such terms do not call for attention in the present series. But there are other terms which cannot be made familiar by means of compact definitions. Students need to grow accustomed to them through simple and straightforward but reasonably full discussions. The purpose of this series is to provide such discussions.

Many critics have borrowed methods and criteria from currently influential bodies of knowledge or belief that have developed without particular reference to literature. In our own century, some of them have drawn on art-history, psychology, or sociology. Others, strong in a comprehensive faith, have looked at literature from a Marxist or a Christian or some other sharply defined point of view. The result has been the importation into literary criticism of terms from the vocabularies of these sciences and creeds. Discussions of such bodies of knowledge and belief in their bearing upon literature and literary criticism form a natural extension of the initial aim of the Critical Idiom.

Because of their diversity of subject-matter, the studies in the series vary considerably in structure. But all the authors have tried to give as full illustrative quotation as possible, to make reference whenever appropriate to more than one literature, and to write in such a way as to guide readers towards the short bibliographies in which they have made suggestions for further reading.

John D. Jump

University of Manchester

1

Introduction

What is myth? 'I know very well what it is, provided that
nobody asks me; but if I am asked and try to explain, I am
baffled.' So wrote St Augustine in his *Confessions* (xi. 14),
grappling engagingly with that elusive category called time,
and anticipating the predicament of anybody who is pressed
for a brief and comprehensive definition of myth. It is the
question itself, we come to realize, which is at fault, for we
have no direct experience of myth as such, but only of particular myths: and these, we discover, are obscure in origin,
protean in form and ambiguous in meaning. Seemingly
immune to rational explication, they nevertheless stimulate
rational enquiry, which accounts for the diversity of conflicting
explanations, none of which is ever comprehensive enough to
explain myth away. Myths partake of that quality ascribed to
poetry in Wallace Stevens' meticulously evasive aphorism:
they appear to resist the intelligence almost successfully. This
is why they attract systematizers who reassure us that the
mighty maze is not without a plan, because myth is nothing
more than primitive science, or history, or the embodiment
of unconscious fantasies, or some other solvent currently in
favour. Evidence adduced in support of each claim often
convinces one that certain myths must have arisen exactly as
the systematizer describes: his skeleton-key undoubtedly fits a
certain type of lock. But systematizers are not content to
contribute one more mythogony to the existent stock, nor to
aspire towards that condition of pluralistic tolerance advocated
by Melville and Frances Herskovits (1958, p. 121); on the

contrary, they are out to discover a comprehensive mono-mythogony of their own, some universal key to all mythologies. George Eliot caricatured their mentality in the person of Casaubon in *Middlemarch* (1871–2), but it would be wrong to deride their single-mindedness, for each of them is the inventor of one of those possibilities which now constitute our range of choice. Resolutely monistic in their approach (and ever prone to the *pars pro toto* fallacy, the hypostatizing of a method into an absolute, and other text-book errors of logic), they avert their gaze from those very exceptions and anomalies which will command the attention of the next investigator, or the one after that. Yet their initial insights are strokes of genius.

Mythogonies are invented by people who cannot bring themselves to accept Malinowski's view that myths simply mean what they say (1926, p. 79). On the contrary, mythogonists habitually assume that a myth conceals a 'real' meaning beneath its apparent meaning. They are generally innocent of the possibility that any tale may have purposive meanings which do not coincide with the purposeful intentions of the teller; and so they regard the intended meaning as the real meaning which their method (and their method alone) is capable of uncovering. They have equally little time for the simplistic view that myths are intended to elicit wonder. Mythogonists, like Poundian exegetes, are much more at ease when unscrewing the inscrutable. What a myth really means, they tell us, may have been lost accidentally through the hazards of oral transmission; or it may have been hidden deliberately by mythmakers reluctant to tell all they know; or it may have been tampered with by political or religious revisionists who produce what Robert Graves calls 'mytho-tropic' versions of stories originally quite different in meaning (1961, p. 219). Alert to such possibilities, they probe the hidden depths, hoping (like all deep-sea divers) to avoid the hallucinations consequent upon nitrogen narcosis.

It was Voltaire's opinion that the study of myths is an occupation for blockheads. Anybody who studies the study of myths, as I do here, must accordingly tremble to know precisely what qualifications he should bring to the task. Is one expected to be able to survey the field with magisterial superciliousness and compile a mythographic appendix to the Earl of Dorset's *Faithful Catalogue of Our Most Eminent Ninnies* (1683)? Or is it enough to prove oneself a superlative blockhead in being willing to undertake such a useless investigation? Hopefully neither. Mythology is a subject in its own right, although not recognized as such in our educational system. Nobody ever gets a B.A. in Mythology. Instead, we assume it to lie within the province of a variety of disciplines such as classics, anthropology, folklore, history of religions, linguistics, psychology and art-history. Each looks at mythology in the light of its own preoccupations, which means that an inquisitive outsider who drifts promiscuously from one to another is likely to conclude that the various specialists are not really talking about the same thing at all, but about different things under the same name. Simply to catalogue the nuances of the word 'myth' and its cognates (*mythos, mythus, mythologem*, etc.) would be a major undertaking; and although White (1972) has made a creditable attempt to produce working definitions of some of these terms for the benefit of literary critics, it is unlikely that others will respect his distinctions, for people engaged in literary studies seem to resent having their terminology refined to several decimal places. I have not made it my business here either to respect the autonomy of mythology (in whatever form it may be thought to exist) or to reconcile with one another the various theories concerning it. I offer instead a partial view of a vast and amorphous topic, and treat mythology as being important primarily on account of its associations with literature. This book is intended for those who are more familiar with English than with any other literature, but who recognize that because

English literature is made by people who read other literatures and absorb ideas from a variety of disciplines, it is sometimes necessary to look far afield in order to understand what goes on at home.

But enough of all this. Let us be guided by J. A. Symonds' somewhat frivolous remark that myths are 'everlastingly elastic' (1890, p. 147) and look now at some of the major theories concerning their nature and provenance. And let us remember that nearly all these approaches have at one time or another seemed so very plausible as to influence the ways in which writers themselves have treated myths in their own poems, plays and novels. Whatever their intrinsic value, therefore, these theories merit attention through having left indelible imprints on our literature.

2

Myths and Theorists

Euhemerism

Some time in the fourth century B.C., a Sicilian called Euhemerus wrote a *Sacred History* in which he describes a visit to an imaginary island called Panchaea, somewhere in the Indian Ocean. Here he learns from an inscription inside the Temple of Zeus that Zeus was a Cretan by birth who travelled in the east and was acclaimed a god there before returning home and dying in Crete. The whole of Euhemerus' novel has not survived in the original or in the Latin translation by Ennius, and the account of it by a fellow Sicilian of the first century B.C., Diodorus Siculus, is also lost. What we know of Euhemerus derives mainly from the *Historia Ecclesiastica* which Eusebius completed early in the fourth century A.D. Attempted reconstructions of Euhemerus' original intentions have to be conducted, therefore, at two removes from what he actually wrote (Eusebius quoting Diodorus quoting Euhemerus), and conflicting conjectures are understandably inevitable. Was Euhemerus being satirical at the expense of Alexander the Great's experiences in India, and cynically recommending self-deification as a means to political ends? Or was he rather the Voltaire or Fontenelle of his day, the man held responsible by Plutarch for having 'disseminated atheism all over the world' (*Moralia*, 360A)? Either way, he is assumed to have written ironically, for the possibility that Euhemerus intended to promote emperor-worship by establishing a distinguished precedent for it has not proved popular among readers who would much prefer an iconoclastic to an imperialistic *Sacred*

History. Whatever his intentions, however, Euhemerus has been credited with spectacular achievements, ranging from the subversion of pagan religions to the foundation of modern anthropology.

An emergent Christianity gladly exploited the polemical possibilities of Euhemerus' revelation that the supreme god of the pagans had been human, all too human, and in doing so they developed what Bolle calls a *euhemerismus inversus* (1970, p. 23) which differs from the earlier kind in being wholly pejorative. To a second-century Christian like Clement of Alexandria, Euhemerus' testimony was devastatingly final: 'the gods you worship were once men', he said in his *Exhortation to the Heathen* (iv), as if bad news like that would procure a massive defection to Christianity. Pagans, however, were accustomed to more casual relations between human and divine than Christians ever envisaged. To them, apotheosis was not a blasphemy but a possibility, admittedly remote, but nevertheless a possibility and therefore an incentive to philanthropic endeavour. That gods were benefactors whose gifts made civilization possible was the opinion of Prodicus of Ceos (fifth century B.C.), who noted the association of bread with Demeter and wine with Dionysus; and lists of divine benefactions were still being compiled a couple of thousand years later when Polydore Virgil wrote his *De Rerum Inventoribus* (Venice, 1499), much to the amusement of John Donne, who chides pagans in *The Second Anniversary* (1612) for their pitiable lack of discrimination in manufacturing gods out of 'agues . . . and war' as well as such domestic commodities as 'wine, and corn, and onions' (lines 425–8). Hercules, Aesculapius, Castor and Pollux, all began life as mortals, as Cicero freely admits (*De Natura Deorum*, ii. 24); Julius Caesar was declared a god of the Roman state after his murder in 44 B.C.

Clement was more than willing to believe that the whole pagan pantheon had been recruited in this way. Early Christians were appalled of course by the polytheistic and idolatrous nature of pagan religions. The Lord their God was a jealous God with an aversion to syndicates. 'Thou shalt have none other gods before me', he decreed, instructing the faithful to kill any of their immediate family who whored after strange gods (Deuteronomy, 13: 6–10); and a passage in the apocryphal *Book of Wisdom* (14: 15–21) warns how fearfully easy it is to commit spiritual fornication with the best of intentions. So perhaps it was inevitable that Reformation polemicists in search of propaganda against egregious popish impostures should avail themselves of euhemeristic arguments in accusing Roman Catholics of resuscitating paganism by practising idolatry; and as late as the eighteenth century Nicolas Fréret acutely drew attention to the persistence among Protestant mythographers of an insidious alliance between euhemerism and anti-Catholicism (Manuel, 1963, p. 96). Later still, and equally controversially, euhemerism was to motivate Herbert Spencer's theory that 'ancestor-worship is the root of every religion' (*The Principles of Sociology* [London, 1882], i. 440).

Euhemerists whose bias was professedly more historical than theological brought a rather different set of questions to bear on the data of pagan mythology. Euhemerism incorporated what Fontenrose calls Palaiphatism (1971, p. 23), after Palaiphatus, who attempted in *De Incredibilibus* (fourth century B.C.) to convert mythic into possible events, and circulated the well-known story that Actaeon was not eaten by his hounds but by debts incurred from extravagant hunting. Once the principle is accepted, stories become histories, and it is only a matter of time before an entomologist may be called upon to testify that Little Miss Muffet (who sat on a tuffet) is none other than the squeamish daughter of Thomas Moufet, author of *The Theatre of Insects* (London, 1658). Taking it for granted that Zeus and all the rest of them had once been mortal, a euhemerist historian felt obliged to determine the dates at which they had lived, in the hope that every major episode recorded in pagan mythology might be placed eventually within the compass of Hebrew history, which was assumed to be the axis of world chronology. As the chronology of antiquity became more refined, increasingly bizarre efforts were made to attach precise dates to episodes embalmed in myths, often by means of some such internal evidence as the mention of a datable astronomical event like the appearance of a comet or an eclipse. The use of astronomical dating as a method for rectifying world chronology on literary evidence was advocated by Joseph Justice Scaliger in his book *De Emendatione Temporum* (Paris, 1583), and the most celebrated English example of the genre is Isaac Newton's *Chronology of the Ancient Kingdoms Emended* (London, 1728), which sets out to preserve the priority of Hebrew civilization by proving that the Greeks have greatly exaggerated the antiquity of their traditions. Euhemerists who believed that Ceres was deified for having taught graniculture to grateful Greeks were now informed that this event had taken place in 1030 B.C. Perseus rescued Andromeda in the year 1005; Theseus killed the Minotaur in 968; Helle drowned in the Hellespont ('so named from her') in 962; Prometheus was unbound in 937.

That people make history by first making myths seemed axiomatic to Niccolo Machiavelli after analyzing ancient Roman power-struggles, and the basic principles of such enterprises were reaffirmed in the Nazi ideology Alfred Rosenberg created in *Der Mythus des 20. Jahrhunderts* (München, 1930). Although the concept is totalitarian it is not particularly modern, in so far as Plato's myths are aimed at subordinating individuals to the desires of the state, and Aristotle thought it likely that this is really what myths are for (*Metaphysics*, xi. 8). Is it so surprising, then, that Francis Bacon should have learned a lesson in counter-revolutionary tactics from studying the story of how Jupiter regained control over Typhon with Mercury's assistance (*The Wisdom of the Ancients* [1619], ch. 2)? The politicization of myth is seen most strikingly in the creation of ethnogenic fables which enable the politically ambitious to declare themselves heirs of antiquity. The significance of the legendary Aeneas to the emperor Augustus is a case in point; so too is the Merovingian myth that the Trojan Francus is the eponymous hero of the Franks. Tudor historiography, as reconstructed by Greenlaw, provides a rich literary yield as well as a classic demonstration of the method, for it was Henry VII who first exploited the British origins of the Welsh Tudor family in ways suggested by a reading of the twelfth-century Geoffrey of Monmouth's fabulous *Historia Regum Britanniae*. Two bits of unfinished business in the matter of Britain – Merlin's prophecy that King Arthur would return eventually to rid Britain of her enemies, and the legend that the land would survive invasions to be ruled once again in the fullness of time by a British monarch – pointed the way to an imaginative man with imperial ambitions: so Henry christened his first son Arthur and hired a mendacious genealogist (André of Toulouse) to trace his line of descent back through the last British king (Cadwallader) to that Trojan Brutus who was allegedly the great-grandson of Aeneas and who eponymously established the brutish British in Albion (Isidore warns us that Britons may have been so called because they are stupid [*bruti*]: *Etymologiae*, ix. 1). *The Faerie Queene* (1590–6) sublimely celebrates on behalf of Queen Elizabeth this Tudor dynastic fantasy which receives much more pedestrian treatment in William Warner's *Albion's England* (1586) and Michael Drayton's *England's Heroical Epistles* (1597); and studies by E. C. Wilson reveal the diligence of imperial mythographers in creating cult-images of Elizabeth (as Astraea, Diana, Pandora, etc.) which could provide a focus and a stimulus for empress-worship. Subsequently, when Elizabeth was dead and the next *Arturius Redivivus*, James I, laid claim to a Divine Right of Kings which placed him above the common law of the land, it became expedient (as Brinkley shows) to replace what Milton called the 'Trojan pretence' of Galfredian British history with a new

Parliamentarian myth of constitutional liberty as manifest in the Saxon legacy of Magna Charta.

Just as myth may be historicized, therefore, so too history can be mythicized by those with a Faulknerian gift for sublimating the actual into the apocryphal. To adopt Peter Munz's terms (1956), the distention of myth into history is complemented by the telescoping of history into myth, in that both processes try to evade the ineffability of isolated events: for seeing that what actually happened (*res gestae*) is knowable only through an account of what happened (*historia rerum gestarum*), the historian becomes a sort of myth-maker willy-nilly. Attempts to dissociate a historical Jesus Christ from the messianic mythology in which he is presented to us are therefore likely to be as absorbingly inconsequential as investigations into the historicity of Robin Hood. But if some myths contain some history, which nobody but a ritualist like Raglan (1936) would deny, then precisely what kind of history is it? Probably what Michael Grant has called 'para-history', which records 'not what happened but what people, at different times, said or believed had happened' (1971, p. xviii). Roman mythology, as Grant reads it, embodies a para-history of Rome; and 'to get an idea of a civilization', he adds, 'one needs a history and a para-history as well.'

Myths as natural science

An alternative to euhemerism is to believe that myths are allegories of goings-on in the universe around us: myths are not history, but natural history. 'All metamorphoses are the physics of the early ages', wrote Fontenelle, echoing Cicero's comment that 'these impious fables enshrined a decidedly clever scientific theory' (*De Natura Deorum*, ii. 24). How was this possible? Mainly because by Cicero's time the names of the gods had long been associated astronomically and

astrologically with the names of planets and zodiacal constel-
lations, as well as geophysically with the names of metals and
the four elements out of which the world was supposed to be
made. How tempting it must have been to look retrospectively
at Greek myths in the light of subsequent developments and
imagine them to have been invented originally by primitive
astrologers or alchemists or other authorities on the arcane.
Christians could dabble in pagan mythology with a clear
conscience provided they remembered (as Sir Walter Ralegh
did) that the names of the pagan gods are really the names of
'natural and divine powers' which God has distributed in the
world for our common benefit (*The History of the World*
[1614], i. 6).

Nobody could doubt the imaginative potential of such
analogical confusion, which enabled writers and artists to
enrich their work with mythological allusions stimulated by
one of the many objects which had a privileged status as an
emblem somewhere or other in the network. Even something
as rudimentary as the procession of the months in Spenser's
Mutability Cantos illustrates this. In rides March upon a ram
('The same which over Hellespontus swam'), followed by
April mounted upon that very bull 'which led/Europa floating
through th'Argolic floods' (vii. 32f); and when the 'lovely
maid' who accompanies August turns out to be no mere stand-
in for Virgo but (on Aratus' authority) Astraea, goddess of
Justice in the Golden Age and cult-image of Queen Elizabeth,
we glimpse various analogies in the process of interlocking
with one another to form elaborately new constructions.

It seemed obvious to George Sandys that Ovid's account of
Venus' adultery with Mars (*Metamorphoses*, iv) was best
understood in the astrological sense as a conjunction of 'hot'
Mars with 'moderate moist' Venus. Pasiphae's affair with a
bull cannot rank among the curiosa of *psychopathia sexualis*
if the bull is really Taurus: all that Pasiphae did, writes
Robert Greene, was to fall in love with astrology (*Planeto-*

machia [London, 1585], p. 22). Following similar hints in Marsilio Ficino's commentary on Plato's *Symposium*, Nesca Robb proposed that the angle at which the lovers lie from one another in Botticelli's painting of Venus and Mars (in the National Gallery) is intended to represent the sextile and trine aspects of their astrological conjunction (Gombrich, 1945, p. 46ff). Was Endymion really only a dedicated moon-watcher, as Robert Greene and a scholiast on Apollonius of Rhodes conjectured? Certainly, pan-Babylonists and solar mythologists figure prominently in the annals of mythological speculation. One thinks of Jacob Bryant's *New System . . . of Ancient Mythology* (London, 1774–6), a book which interested Blake and Coleridge, and which sets out to prove that sun-worship is the key to all pagan mythology. Or of Charles François Dupuis' demonstration in his *Origine de Tous les Cultes* (Paris, 1794) that the zodiac is the matrix of all mythologies, with the Twelve Labours of Hercules denoting 'astronomical realities' as the sun progresses through the zodiacal calendar (the sun enters Leo as Hercules slays the Nemean lion, etc.).

Planet earth attracted its share of attention. The supposition that pagan myths are to be understood as allegories of natural processes here on earth seems to have been entertained as early as the sixth century B.C. by Theagenes of Rhegium. Perhaps embarrassed by Homeric accounts of squabbles on Mount Olympus, Theagenes made sense of what he read by assuming that various deities symbolize natural elements, in which case their disagreements might be accounted for in terms of the theory of Opposites favoured in contemporary physics: the sea-god Poseidon is really water, Apollo fire and Hera air. A century later, when Empedocles wrote his verse-treatise on Nature, all four elements had acquired mythological names: Hera was still the air, but 'bright Zeus' was now fire; earth was represented by Aidoneus (god of the underworld) and water by an unknown and weeping nymph called Nestis.

'Such was the origin of mythology', Holbach concluded in his *Système de la Nature* (London, 1770): 'It may be said to be the daughter of natural philosophy, embellished by poetry, and only destined to describe nature and its parts' (ch. 19). The major problem was to decide whether ancient myths record merely an imaginative response to the natural world (which is roughly the Romantic view), or whether they constitute a rudimentary form of science, not that 'rustic science' mocked by Plato's Socrates in his denunciation of myth (*Phaedrus*, 229) but what Renaissance humanists considered to be the secret wisdom of the Ancients. We encounter the Romantic attitude in Robert Wood, who was among the first to believe that myths might be explained by the geography of their origin. 'When the sun goes down behind the cloud-capped mountains of Macedonia and Thessaly', he writes in *An Essay on the Original Genius and Writings of Homer* (London, 1775), 'there is a picturesque wildness in the appearance, under certain points of view, which naturally calls to mind the old fable of the rebel giants bidding defiance to Jupiter, and scaling the heavens, as the fanciful suggestion of this rugged perspective' (p. 136). If it was not the view which catalyzed mythopoeic processes, then it was probably the weather, especially bad weather. Norse mythology, with its storm-god Woden and its thunder-god Donar, encouraged late Romantic thunder-mythologists like Adalbert Kuhn and Wilhelm Schwartz to reduce mythology to meteorology, as John Ruskin did while examining Greek myths of cloud and storm in *The Queen of the Air* (London, 1869). Max Müller, on the other hand, shifted the emphasis from terror to ecstasy and construed the whole of mythology as an elaborate paean to the dawn (1881, p. 400ff.). All this is very different from Francis Bacon's humanistic approach to nature myths when discussing Pan in *The Wisdom of the Ancients* (London, 1619). Like Boccaccio, Bacon believed that myths embody natural truths, though 'hidden' (Boccaccio warns) 'with an art that will surprise you' (*De*

Genealogia Deorum, xiv. Preface).

Alchemists, those self-styled sons of Hermes, needed no convincing, and searched through Greek and Hebrew mythologies for hermetic doctrines concerning the transformation of metals. In this they were encouraged by the fact that names used for some of the planets were also used for certain metals, which means that a text mentioning Saturn or Mars might be presumed equally plausibly to refer to astronomy proper or to the 'lower astronomy' (*astronomia inferior*) of metallurgy, and be subject to astrological or alchemical interpretations. Concerned as they were with the transmutation of base metals into gold, it was inevitable that they should pay particular attention to the transformations recorded in Ovid's *Metamorphoses*. Daphne's flight from Phoebus Apollo caught the attention of an anonymous contributor to Ashmole's *Theatrum Chemicum Britannicum* (1652), who recognized in it the formula for manufacturing the Philosopher's Stone: mix a moist and volatile Daphne with a hot and dry Phoebus until the mixture solidifies, add a little fresh water, then wash with virgin's milk (p. 420). Gods and goddesses are reduced to chemical properties and given nominal status in the alchemical vocabulary, while their social and sexual intercourse signifies alchemical processes. Ashmole prints another anonymous poem called 'The Hermit's Tale', too long to quote here, which is an alchemical sequel to Venus' adulterous affair with Mars, and illustrates how new adventures could be invented for the pagan deities by those willing to experiment alchemically and publish their findings in mythological terms. Usually, however, it was assumed that the ancient texts themselves contain all one needs to know. Old Testament patriarchs from Adam onwards were believed to have been well informed about alchemy: how else could they have lived so long? Moses calcined the Golden Calf and made a cordial out of the powder for the Children of Israel (Exodus, 32:20); his 'sister' (Maria Prophetissa) wrote a *Practica . . . in Artem Alchemica*, to which Solomon added a *Liber de Lapide*, neither of which is easy to come by, thanks to the efforts of biblical scholars and sceptical chemists. Pagan mythology, on the other hand, posed no such canonical problems, and was rich in possibilities. Why would the Argonauts have risked their lives to obtain the Golden Fleece (*vellus*) had it not been a vellum parchment containing the formula for gold manufacture? After all, the sheep from which the Fleece came had once belonged to Hermes. Or perhaps the Fleece itself was the Stone, and Jason's adventures an account of stages in the alchemical process? Such speculations are recorded as early as the fifth century by John of Antioch and mentioned in the famous *Lexicon* attributed to Suidas in the tenth; and the last major attempt to read ancient mythology as a secret alchemical language was by Antoine Pernety in his *Dictionnaire Mytho-Hermétique* (Paris, 1787). Histories of alchemy reveal just how seriously such readings were taken. There is an *Aureum Vellus* (Rorschach, 1598) by Salomon Trismosin and an unpublished seventeenth-century *Revelation of the Mystery of the Golden Fleece* by Robert Napier; there is also an *Atalanta Fugiens* (Oppenheim, 1618) by Michael Maier and an *Oedipus Chemicus* (Amsterdam, 1664) by Johann Joachim Becher. We tend to think of such works nowadays mainly in connection with Ben Jonson's coruscating comedy *The Alchemist* (1610), which satirizes both practical quackery in the activities of Subtle and the wilder reaches of dilettante speculation in the virtuoso Sir Epicure Mammon. Sir Epicure has read enough to be able to venture the odd contribution to alchemical hermeneutics, which he does in his comments on the founder of Thebes, Cadmus. It was Cadmus, we remember, who sowed the teeth of a dragon he had killed, thus causing to spring up from the ground a number of fully armed men, who were provoked into fighting one another when Cadmus threw a stone amongst them. A barbaric and ridiculous tale? Not to an alchemical adept who sees immediately that this Stone is no ordinary stone, and that what masquerades as myth is really a set of laboratory notes in cipher:

> The dragon's teeth [are] mercury sublimate,
> That keeps the whiteness, hardness, and the biting;
> And they are gathered into Jason's helm
> (The alembic) and then sowed in Mars his field.
>
> (II. i. 96–9)

It is no more complicated to follow than Mrs Beeton, once you accept Sir Epicure's assumption that all references to gold in classical mythology (the apples in the garden of the Hesperides, Jove's epiphany to Danae, the Midas touch) are 'abstract riddles of our Stone', and devote your energies to the business of decoding what has been so skilfully encoded.

People convinced that myths record observations about the natural world often conclude that the purpose of a myth is not simply to describe something but to explain how it came into existence. Frazer thought myths are 'mistaken explanations of phenomena, whether of human life or of external nature' (1921, p. xxvii), with the emphasis of course on *mistaken*. Among distinguished opponents of this aetiological theory of myth one might single out Bronislaw Malinowski, who counters it with the functionalist view that myths do not explain origins but preserve precedents which justify the status quo: myth is 'a pragmatic charter of primitive faith and moral wisdom' (1926, p. 23). R. R. Marett was equally convinced that 'myth is not aetiological but fidejussive. Its business is not to satisfy curiosity but to confirm the faith' (James, 1957, p. 477f.). Ritualists point out that aetiological explanations are invariably *ex post facto* constructions. Perhaps the aetiological theory is so disparaged because it is all too reminiscent of those *Just So Stories* (London, 1902) which Rudyard Kipling wrote for children, explaining how the leopard got his spots and how the camel acquired a hump as punishment for habitually humphing; reminiscent, too, of Joel Chandler Harris' *Uncle*

Remus: His Songs and His Sayings (New York, 1880), which also has its its share of comic aetiologies explaining why negroes are black and why rabbits have short tails. But the stories of Uncle Remus were read carefully by Herbert Huntington Smith, who was busy collecting similar tales among South American Indians long before Claude Lévi-Strauss did the field-work there which obliged him to reject Malinowski's functionalist premises. Poets have always invented aetiological conceits explaining how the lyre came into existence or where Cupid got his bow from (their mistress' eyebrows, usually). Grant finds aetiologies everywhere in Roman mythology (1971, p. 219), thus supporting the first part of H. J. Rose's definition of myth in *The Oxford Classical Dictionary* (Oxford, 1970): 'a pre-scientific and imaginative attempt to explain some phenomenon, real or supposed, which excites the curiosity of the myth-maker.'

The second half of Rose's definition (myth is 'an effort to reach a feeling of satisfaction in place of uneasy bewilderment concerning such phenomena') is by contrast psychological in emphasis; so we must look now at some of the leading psychological explanations of myth.

Psychological approaches

'Can you imagine what "endopsychic myths" are?' Freud asked Wilhelm Fliess in December 1897, a couple of months after introducing him to the theory of the Oedipus complex, which the rest of the world was not to hear about for another three years or so. Happily, Freud decided to explain. 'The dim inner perception of one's own psychical apparatus stimulates illusions which are naturally projected outwards, and characteristically into the future and a world beyond.' Representative illusions produced entirely as a result of psychic projection include our ideas of 'immortality, retribution [and] the world after death', all of which are simply 'reflections of our inner psyche . . . psycho-mythology'. Freud first discovered the operative mechanism of *projection* during his researches into paranoia, which Fliess was told about in January 1895 (*CPW*, i, p. 209) and which was soon to figure in an 1896 paper on the neuropsychoses of defence (*CPW*, iii, p. 184). Five years later, the key to paranoia had been found to unlock mythology as well, for in *The Psychopathology of Everyday Life* (1901) Freud declares unequivocally his belief that 'a large part of the mythological view of the world, which extends a long way into the most modern religions, is *nothing but psychology projected into the external world*' (*CPW*, vi, p. 258). The psychologist's task as envisaged in *Totem and Taboo* (1913) is to 'reverse the process and put back into the human mind what animism teaches us is the nature of things' (*CPW*, xiii, p. 91). Nature mythologists have got it all wrong, for landscapes are really mindscapes ('O the mind, mind has mountains') and are no more objectively existent than the desolate location of Spenser's Cave of Despair, which is an outward and visible manifestation of spiritual death.

Freud looked upon myths as 'precipitates' of unconscious processes (*CPW*, xx, p. 212). Looked at clinically, the story of Narcissus emblematizes a mode of neurotic inversion which Freud first identified as narcissism in a 1910 essay on Leonardo da Vinci (*CPW*, xi, p. 100); and the fate of the man who went blind after peeping at Lady Godiva helped Freud clarify a theory about psychogenic disturbance of vision (*CPW*, xi, p. 217). Even something as grotesque as the Egyptian goddess Mut (vulture-headed, mammiferous, and ithyphallic) offered insights into the bizarre world of infantile sexuality (*CPW*, xi, p. 93f.). At the same time, Freud was prepared to give as well as to receive, and use the knowledge he had already acquired in order to exhume unfamiliar meanings from familiar myths. In backing up Ferenczi's claim that the real horror of the Gorgon Medusa (who had serpentine hair and a petrifying gaze) is that she represents an infantile neurotic impression of female genitalia, Freud stressed the importance of recognizing that it is the mother's genitals which are thus symbolized: 'Athene, who carries Medusa's head on her armour, becomes in consequence the unapproachable woman, the sight of whom extinguishes all thought of a sexual approach' (*CPW*, xix, p. 144; but alas, it was Perseus who severed Medusa's head and gave it to Athene to wear on her breastplate, which makes for unimaginable sexual complications). By the 1930s Freud was producing in all seriousness mythological interpretations which were the envy of his parodists. Who else but Freud would have had the temerity to explain Theseus' adventure in the Cretan labrinth as 'a representation of anal birth: the twisting paths are the bowels and Ariadne's thread is the umbilical cord' (*CPW*, xxii, p. 25)? Or say that Prometheus managed to keep fire in a phallic fennel-stalk by continently witholding the fluid which would have extinguished it (*CPW*, xxii, p. 187–93)?

If myths are projections, what part of the mind are they projected from? Freud assumed it was from the unconscious, which he imagined as a sort of cellar in which are stored sexual fantasies the conscious mind would rather not know about: consequently, in Freud's view, myths are as sex-ridden as R. P. Knight had surmised in his *Discourse on the Worship of Priapus* (London, 1786). Jung disagreed. Initially, he accepted the theory of projection, but later modified it by conceiving of the unconscious mind as 'ecphorating' (i.e. 'carrying forth') primordial images rather than simply casting them out (*CW*, ix(1), p. 25; xvi, p. 122). A more radical move, however, was Jung's decision to reject Freud's model of the unconscious, and to substitute a two-tiered structure of his own design. The upper level is the 'personal unconscious' which lies just below the threshold of consciousness and is a receptacle for repressions, just as Freud said it was: it is this 'personal unconscious' which is susceptible to Freudian analysis.

But beneath this lies a much deeper 'collective unconscious' whose secrets cannot be opened up by the techniques of Freudian analysis (slips of the tongue, word-association tests, symbol-detection) because its contents were never suppressed in the first place. This collective unconscious is universal, 'identical in all men, and thus constitutes a common psychic substrate of a suprapersonal nature which is present in every one of us' (*CW*, ix(1), p. 3–4). Jung first called the contents of the collective unconscious 'archetypes' in 1919, and it is these which produce those 'archetypal images' familiar in myths, dreams, art and literature, 'universal images that have existed since the remotest times' (ibid., p. 4–5). Jung's distinction between *archetype* and *archetypal image* is important in view of the way literary critics often confuse the two. 'The term "archetype",' Jung explains, 'is not meant to denote an inherited idea, but rather an inherited mode of functioning corresponding to the inborn way in which the chick emerges from the egg' (Jacobi, 1959, p. 43). What we encounter in myths and literature are merely archetypal images. It is not the images themselves which we inherit biologically in the structure of our brain-cells, but the capacity for making such images: 'there are no inborn ideas, but there are inborn possibilities of ideas that set bounds to even the boldest fantasy' (*CW*, xv, p. 81). Jung claimed that his researches had 'opened up a field of psychic phenomena which are themselves the matrix of all mythology', specifically 'archetypes like the anima, animus, wise old man, witch, shadow, earth-mother, etc., and the organizing dominants, the self, the circle, and the quaternity' (*CW*, v, p. 390f.). Whatever Freud may say, mythology is 'collective psyche, and not individual psyche' (*CW*, vii, p. 91f.), which is why the ancient myths were psycho-therapeutic to the people who believed in them: 'they explained to the bewildered human being what was going on in his unconscious and why he was held fast' (*CW*, v, p. 308). When rationalism prevailed and people grew too sophisticated to believe in myths, the psychic powers those myths had once identified and harnessed got dangerously out of control, with the devastating effects evoked in Auden's poem 'A New Age':

> The vanquished powers were glad
> To be invisible and free; without remorse
> Struck down the sons who strayed into their course,
> And ravished the daughters, and drove the fathers mad.

The whole theory strikingly illustrates what Whitehead used to call the Fallacy of Misplaced Concreteness, for Jung's 'collective unconscious' is no more empirically verifiable than Noam Chomsky's 'deep structure', which similarly appears to explain everything except itself.

For all their differences, however, Freud and Jung share the same affectivist assumptions when explaining our fascination with mythic materials. Each assumes that we somehow know what a myth is telling us, long before we know that we know. In Freud's case, the theory of the Oedipus complex emerged as much from a study of audience reactions to *Oedipus Rex* as from an understanding of the formal properties of Sophocles' play. Oedipus' fate, we learn, 'moves us only because it might have been ours', for *Oedipus Rex* enacts a major recognition-scene for the benefit of our unconscious; so there we all sit in fascinated horror while Oedipus acts out the 'primeval wishes of our childhood' (*CPW*, iv, p. 262). The force which draws us to this play (as to *Hamlet*) operates at a subliminal level, for a playwright can be no more aware than his audience of why he should find this kind of subject-matter so compulsively fascinating. Even more importance is attached to the affective element in myth by Jung, who testifies that 'when an archetypal situation occurs we suddenly feel an extraordinary sense of release, as though transported, or caught up by an overwhelming power. At such moments we are no longer individuals, but the race; the voice of all mankind resounds in us' (*CW*, xv, p. 82). The critical perils of an over-reliance on such shocks of recognition are displayed in *Archetypal Patterns in Poetry* (London, 1934), by the Jungian critic Maud Bodkin. Her method, best illustrated in her analysis of Coleridge's 'Rime of the Ancient Mariner', is to scan works of literature seismographically for mythic tremors. When she reads that the shadow of the becalmed ship 'burnt alway/A still and awful red', she finds that the word *red* 'has a soul of terror that has come to it through the history of the race' (p. 44). A Freudian psychologist would want to know how she could be so sure that her reaction to *red* is not simply due to some personal trauma; a literary critic, on the other hand, would be inclined to attribute her reaction to the local context of Coleridge's poem, and ask whether she had ever felt stirrings of racial terror when reading Burns's poem 'My Love is Like a Red Red Rose'.

The rediscovery of mythology as an encyclopedia of psychological types and universal emotions stimulated writers to take a new interest in the old myths. Early chapters of Frederick J. Hoffman's book on *Freudianism and the Literary Mind* (Baton Rouge, 1957) trace the diaspora of Freudian ideas among British and American writers, but we have no comparable study of Jung's influence. On the face of it, one would think that Jung has much more to offer writers than Freud, for the emotional range encompassed by his theory of archetypes is so much greater than the narrowly sexual emphasis of Freudian readings. 'Whoever speaks in primordial images speaks with a thousand voices', writes Jung (*CW*, xv, p. 82). Yeats reached similar conclusions independently, for in an essay on 'Magic' (1901) he expressed his belief in the existence of a Great Memory clearly akin to the Jungian collective unconscious, although developed from the *Anima Mundi* as imagined by the seventeenth-century Platonist Henry More. 'Whatever the passions of man have gathered about', according to Yeats, 'becomes a symbol in the Great

Memory, and in the hands of him who has the secret it is a worker of wonders, a caller-up of angels or of devils' (*Essays and Introductions* [London, 1961], pp. 28, 50). *A Vision* (London, 1937) reveals the eclectic nature of Yeats's search for archetypal images like that of the 'rough beast' in his poem 'The Second Coming', which slouches towards its Bethlehem to be born. For Yeats as for Jung, images which evoke primordial emotions are the means to a literature of universal significance.

Jung's theory of archetypal images is a controversial way of looking at the old and still unsolved problem of how it comes about that societies remote from one another in time and place may nevertheless invent pretty much the same stories. To put it like that is of course to beg the whole question, for what is at issue is whether or not myths allegedly 'universal' or 'eternally recurrent' are actually or only relatively so: are we confronted by absolute identities or mere family resemblances?

Those who believe that similarities outweigh differences can do one of two things. They may, on the one hand, favour the uniformitarian hypothesis that all myths are the same because all men are the same, in which case similarities are only to be expected. On the other hand, they may believe their favourite mythology is the most ancient and venerable known to man, and see evidence of cultural diffusion or downright plagiarism in similarities between their own and some other mythology. In times when Justin Martyr felt obliged to prove that the virgin birth of Perseus had not inspired the virgin birth of Jesus Christ (*Dialogue with Trypho*, lxvii–lxx), and when Celsus was able find nothing but warped versions of Plato in Christian doctrines, Clement of Alexandria could simply reverse the charges in his *Miscellanies* (i. 22) by quoting Numenius: 'what is Plato, but Moses speaking in Attic Greek?' So was born the comforting fiction, promulgated in Justin Martyr's *Hortatory Address to the Greeks* (xiv), that Homer and Plato had both visited Egypt and there picked up a good deal of Mosaic lore which is still discernible (though corrupt) in Greek literature. This is the Christian commonplace to which Giles Fletcher alludes in his poem on *Christ's Triumph Over and After Death* (Cambridge, 1610):

> Who doth not see drowned in Deucalion's name
> (When earth his men, and sea had lost his shore)
> Old Noah; and in Ninus' lock, the fame
> Of Samson yet alive . . . ?

(st. 7)

Sceptics focus on anomalies which form-finders overlook and conclude that similarity is an illusion created by selectivity. If myths were truly universal, they say, we might expect cosmogonies and autochthonies to be the same all over the world. The problem, as Frankfort sees it (1958, p. 168), is not to explain how Greeks and Tamanacs quite independently of one another came to conceive of humanity as having developed out of stones thrown backwards, but to explain why it is that no other people should have hit upon such an origin. When Lessa looked for the Oedipus myth among Pacific islanders he was unable to find a single instance in which all three basic in- gredients (prophecy, parricide and incest) were present. Christians like Ong who believe that time is linear and unique are naturally opposed to all universalist theories which imply circularity and repetition, like those described by Mircea Eliade in *The Myth of the Eternal Return* (New York, 1954). 'In the cosmos as we know it,' writes Ong, 'there is no real repetition anywhere, for all is in active evolution. One sees repetition only in the rough, when one does not examine more closely' (1967, p. 311).

Time and again one senses, in controversies concerning the psychoanalytic approach to myth, that mere evidence will never settle the issue one way or another, because the real subject of concern is anxiety about the nature of the mytho- poeic imagination: is it, as we like to believe, an expression of our freedom to invent alternative realities, or is it merely an agent of those powerful forces (personal and traumatic, or racial and primordial) which determine our lives?

Moral didactics

Among the rigours to which Byron's Don Juan was subject at an impressionable age was a classical education, which caused his mother no end of worry. For despite her enormous respect for classical antiquities, Donna Inez 'dreaded the Mythology' – that *chronique scandaleuse* of gods and goddesses, who 'never put on pantaloons or bodices' (*Don Juan*, i. 41); and of course her fears were well-founded, for the precocious boy whose favourite reading was centos of salacious passages from bowdlerized texts was not entirely unprepared for the day when his pretty young tutor tentatively gave him 'a pure Platonic squeeze' (i. 91). Donna Inez' predicament is traditionally that of the Christian humanist who believes on the one hand that an education which ignores the classics is no education at all, but who fears on the other hand that classical literature has a tendency to deprave and corrupt if read indiscriminately. Its polytheism makes it potentially subversive to the Christian faith, and its moral code leaves much to be desired. 'The Greek gods are rakes, and unnatural rakes', Gerard Manley Hopkins complained to Dixon (23 October 1886): 'they have no manners, they are not gentlemen . . .'

It stood to reason, however, that if the Greeks had cribbed their mythology from Moses, pagan myths must inevitably retain vestiges of the true faith. Boccaccio, who believed that 'pagan poets had an imperfect sense of the true God' (*De Genealogia Deorum*, xiv. 13), was guided by St Paul's remark that 'whatsoever things were written aforetime were written for our learning' (Romans, 15:4). So too was the author of the fourteenth-century *Ovide Moralisé*, a poem which rolls along for seven-and-a-half thousand lines after a preliminary push from St Paul: 'Se l'escripture ne me ment,/Tout est pour nostre enseignement.' Justification could be found also in the fact that God condoned the looting of Egyptian property by the Children of Israel (Exodus, 12:35f.); for if this is interpreted to mean that the products of paganism are uncontaminated by the spirit of paganism, Christians are free to take whatever they fancy, as Hawkins observed when gathering emblems for *Parthenia Sacra* (Rouen, 1633). Allegory was the inevitable go-between, because both pagans and Christians were accustomed to read their own mythologies allegorically. St Paul explained to the Galatians (4:22–31) that the Genesis story of Abraham and his two sons ('one by a bondmaid, the other by a freewoman') is really an allegory of the twin covenants of Law and Grace; and Philo Judaeus used complex allegories in an attempt to redeem what he considered to be absurdities in the book of Genesis. By the time that a pagan epithalamy now known to us as The Song of Solomon had been explained by Origen as an allegory of Christ's mystic marriage with the Church, it was too late to call off the search for spiritual meanings in unlikely places.

As for the pagan tradition, the allegorizing of Homer had begun in the sixth century B.C. with Theagenes of Rhegium, who believed that some of the Homeric characters are really personified qualities. If you think (as he did) that Athene 'is' wisdom, Ares folly, Aphrodite desire and Hermes reason, you are soon drawn to the Stoic conclusion that mythology is a non-discursive form of ethical teaching, and start looking out for those moral allegories which figure so prominently in George Sandys' notes to his 1632 translation of Ovid's *Metamorphoses*. Prodicus' Hercules, who stands at the crossroads and contemplates the broad way to Vice before taking the rough road to Virtue, is neither man nor god but Wisdom caught in the very act of making a correct moral choice (Xenophon, *Memorabilia*, ii. 1). Even Pope felt obliged to add moral appendices to his translations of Homer for the benefit of busy moralists who might want to lay their hands quickly upon an example of Prudence Restraining Passion in the *Iliad*, or of Virgin Modesty Commended in the *Odyssey*. And if one happened to believe that mythology is not only a comprehensive 'sociology of morals' (Vickers, 1973, p. 261) but also a secret philosophical system, allegoresis was a means of reclaiming the lost wisdom of the Ancients. Before Vico finally demolished the theory in his *Scienza Nuova* (1725–44, paragraph 384), it was axiomatic to mythographers like Natale Conti that the Ancients had embodied their philosophical doctrines in myths (*Mythologiae* [1567], Book x): *quod omnia philosophorum dogmata sub fabulis continebantur* was a message taken very much to heart by Francis Bacon when reporting his own mythographic researches in *The Wisdom of the Ancients* (1619), which Garner claims is Bacon's most complex and concise philosophical work (1970, p. 280), and certainly not the anachronism it is usually taken to be. In the excitement of the hunt for occult philosophies, nobody was put off by Seneca's warning that works of literature contain many philosophies but no philosophy. Seneca was amused at the way Stoics and Epicureans, Peripatetics and Academics, all imputed their conflicting doctrines to the Homeric poems. The conclusion was obvious: 'no one of these doctrines is to be fathered upon Homer, just because they are all there' (*Epistulae*, lxxxviii. 5).

Theoretically, it was assumed that every myth is encased in a verbal covering (*integumentum*) which is probably quite different from the core meaning underneath. The integument is fictive, but the core is true: allegoresis, as George Chapman understood it when translating the *Odyssey*, involves removing the fictive integument in order to uncover 'the most material and doctrinal illation of Truth'. In this way even Ovid could be given the benefit of the doubt: the *Metamorphoses* may look merely fabulous, notes William Webbe in his *Discourse of English Poetry* (London, 1586), 'yet being moralized according to his meaning [i.e. intention], and the truth of every tale being discovered, it is a work of exceeding wisdom and sound judgment' (p. 29). Everything is passed through the same moral filter and emerges as an *exemplum* of something or other. If Jupiter assumes the semblance of a bull or if Apuleius is transformed into an ass, this can only mean 'that a man once given over to his lust . . . is no better than a beast' (Robert Burton, *The Anatomy of Melancholy* [London, 1652], iii. 2. 3). Sin is bestial, so each of Spenser's Seven Deadly Sins rides an appropriate beast; Gluttony is drawn after the manner of Silenus, because pagan gods exemplify various aspects of human degradation. What made the moralizing method so very tenacious was its tolerance of antithetical interpretations which record positive and negative lessons to be learned from the same phenomenon. Leander's swim across the Hellespont to join Hero may be read accordingly *in bono* or *in malo*; *in bono* it signifies the Christian soul struggling to reach divine sapience; *in malo*, Leander's death by drowning shows that people who devote themselves to mere earthly love get their just deserts (*Ovide Moralisé*, 3587–731).

Critics of the moralistic approach complained that it made neither good theology nor good sense to scour pagan myths for Christian messages. Extremists thought it dangerous to tamper with pagan poetry at all, on the grounds that 'he that toucheth pitch, shall be defiled therewith' (Ecclesiasticus, 13:1). John Walton prefaced his translation of Boethius in the early fifteenth century with the caveat that pagan materials are out of bounds to good Christians:

> Nought liketh me to labour nor to muse
> Upon these old poesies dark;
> For Christ's faith such things should refuse,
> Witness upon Jerome, the holy clerk:
> It should not be a Christian man's work
> The false gods' names to renew . . .

Nor were the testimonies of pagan writers made use of as corroboratory evidence by biblical commentators. The trouble was that pagans could be made to look deceptively virtuous if they were known only through mosaics of quotations in *florilegia* carefully culled by educated Christians. Erasmus even went so far as to say in his *Enchiridion Militis Christiani* (Basel, 1518) that more religion is to be found in some of the moralized myths (he instances the stories of Circe, Tantalus, Sisyphus and the Labours of Hercules) than in a literal reading of the Bible itself. What had happened during the reign of Julian the Apostate in the fourth century stood as an awful reminder of the threat posed by a refined paganism to established Christianity; and it is significant that when the Church issued its Tridentine *Index Librorum Prohibitorum* in 1564 it listed the *Ovidius Moralizatus* and not the original works of Ovid (Seznec, 1953, p. 274f).

Other critics found moralized mythology not so much dangerous as downright stupid, as Luther did in his commentary on Genesis (Allen, 1970, p. 240). St Augustine seemed to think that the morality of pagan myths was no more in evidence than the emperor's new clothes. If anybody believes that such tales inculcate morality, he mocked, 'let him tell in what places the gods taught these precepts' (*De Civitas Dei*, ii. 6). Can a pious fable, and a dirty story, share in the total literary glory? Rabelais, whose competence in one of these genres is beyond reproach, was inclined to think not, and accused the moralizers of perpetrating a gigantic con-game. 'Do you honestly believe', he asked in his prologue to *Gargantua* (1534), 'that Homer, penning his *Iliad* or *Odyssey*, ever dreamed of the allegorical patchwork subsequently inflicted upon him . . . ? Homer no more dreamed of all this allegorical fustian than Ovid in his *Metamorphoses* dreamed of the Gospel.' Were the moralizers ever conscious of their attempt to fool all of the people all of the time? Or were they guilty only of self-deception in anaesthetizing their moral consciences before indulging in the sensuous and sometimes sensual pleasures afforded by mythology? On the pedestal of Bernini's lovely statue of Apollo and Daphne is a motto, the gist of which is that transient love-affairs get you nowhere, the implication being that this is what the statue portrays. You forget the motto the very moment your eyes encounter those exquisite bodies, but it is always there in a moral emergency. But for the naiveties or hypocrisies of assiduous moralizers, how much pagan mythology would have survived the destructive attention of pious Christians?

Language games

Now that we have given up hunting beavers for pharmaceutical purposes, no modern naturalist ever gets a chance to observe the beaver's extraordinary habit of biting off his own testicles in order to elude capture. Medieval beavers, it appears, were acutely aware of their importance in the economy as primary producers of castoreum, an unctuous substance secreted in their groins and used in the preparation of medicines and perfumes; so when the hunt closed in, they would castrate themselves in the knowledge that their pursuers would then leave them alone. This much we learn from a delightful Latin bestiary of the twelfth century translated by T. H. White as *The Book of Beasts* (London, 1954), where the beaver is called by his Latin name, Castor (p. 28). This explains everything. Beavers are so-called because they castrate themselves, Isidore writes: *castores a castrando* (*Etymologiae*, xii. 2). Nobody knows exactly how this myth concerning the beaver first came to be circulated, but one thing is fairly certain: whoever invented the story had never looked very closely at beavers, for if he had, he would have discovered that the male beaver's testicles are internal and cannot possibly be bitten off (or perhaps he *did* look, and concluded that every specimen which came to hand was already the victim of a previous hunt). What probably happened was that the myth was invented in order to explain the beaver's Latin name, the logic here being exactly the same as that which determined the name of the Mock Turtle's schoolteacher: 'we called him Tortoise because he taught us' (or conversely, with a name like that, how could the tortoise have been anything but a schoolteacher?). 'Names and natures do often agree', says the proverb. Formal analysis of this supposition begins with Plato's *Cratylus*, which examines the problem of whether the names we attach to things are merely conventional labels (the opinion of Hermogenes and most modern linguists) or whether names are chosen originally because they represent the nature of the things they describe (which is what Cratylus and the majority of poets and novelists believe). If you agree with Cratylus that names are organic with the things they denote, then you will be tempted to search language for information about reality, and probe the world of words for insights into the world of things. The fact that language changes is no problem at all provided you are willing to conduct your enquiries etymologically: all you need to do is to ascertain the direction of the semantic drift by examining earlier usages, and then paddle upstream to the source, where you will find that pristine etymon which miraculously *is* what it describes. The clue to Castor's nature is Castor's name.

We now think differently, of course. Cassirer (1946, p. 31) illustrates the way in which language denotes only our conception of objects (and not the objects themselves) by contrasting the Greek and Latin words for 'moon': to Greeks, the moon was the 'measuring one' (μήν), whereas to the Romans it was *luna*, the 'shining one'. Mythmakers are generally incapable of that kind of discrimination. If our bestiary-writer is less than helpful as a naturalist, he at least shows us one of the ways in which a myth may originate. Consider, for example, the myth very often encountered in

Platonist poetry of how the soul languishes in the prison of the body and yearns for the day when death will release it: this seems to have been promoted by curiosity about the similarity between the Greek words for body (σῶμα) and tomb (σῆμα). Plato draws attention to this in his *Cratylus* (400) and again in *Phaedo* (62), where this time the tomb is replaced by a prison (φρουρά). This is most illuminating, because here the change of word obscures the verbal origin of the idea, and the myth is cut loose from its moorings in the Greek language to drift independently. The story of how Samson found honey in the carcase of the lion he had killed (Judges, 14:8) turns out to be only a way of saying that the Hebrew word for 'honey' is derived from the Hebrew word for 'lion' (Porter); and the Greek myth of how Deucalion and his wife Pyrrha repopulated the earth after the Flood by throwing stones behind them is less puzzling once Sandys has explained (p. 70) that the Greek word for 'stone' (λαός) is remarkably similar to the word for 'people' (λᾶας). It may be nonsense, but it is the kind of nonsense from which some myths were probably made before philologists finally proved it to be nonsense.

Even so, a surprisingly large number of verbally inspired myths have managed to survive the scrutiny of modern philologists. A linguistic origin is still alleged for the story of how God multiplied the languages of those engaged in building the tower of Babel, thus frustrating their impious endeavour to reach heaven. It all began with a linguistic attempt to explain the ziggurats of Babylon (Babil) by means of the Hebrew *balal* ('to confuse'): 'therefore is the name of it called Babel; because the Lord did there confound the language of all the earth' (Genesis, 11:9). And if English poetry from Spenser to Shelley resounds with 'the dreaded name/ Of Demogorgon' (*Paradise Lost*, ii. 964f.), ultimate ancestor of all the gods although a deity completely unknown to the Ancients, we now know that this is largely because Boccaccio perpetuated the misreading of δημιουργός ('demiurge, creator') as Demogorgon, an error first committed by the scholiast on Statius' *Thebaid* (iv. 516).

What the nineteenth century came to know as the 'science' of mythology developed from the hypothesis of a new primitive language (first called Aryan, and later Indo-European) from which Sanskrit, Greek and Latin were all descended, as Sir William Jones originally suggested in 1786. By means of what Friedrich Schlegel was soon to call 'comparative grammar' (1808), the probable structure of this *Ursprache* was worked out; and Grimm's Law (1822) and Verner's Law (1875) explained the sound-changes which had taken every language descended from Indo-European along its separate path. For the first time ever it became possible to determine whether verbal similarities in different languages were purely accidental or cognate forms within the one great family. The exciting implications of all this for mythological studies are still vibrant in a book-length essay on 'Comparative Mythology' (1856) by the much-maligned F. Max Müller, who believed that 'the mythology of the Veda is to comparative mythology what Sanskrit has been to comparative grammar' (1881, p. 381). Müller's achievement was to bring the methods of comparative philology to bear upon the old suspicion that myths originate in some sort of word-play. He believed that the Aryans had expressed their observations of nature anthropomorphically in metaphorical language. Not having reached that level of abstraction which would have enabled them to say something as simple as 'it is night', they found themselves obliged to say that 'Selene kisses Endymion into sleep' (everybody knowing that Selene was what we would call the moon and Endymion the setting sun). When the Aryan tribes dispersed into what later became Europe, they took their metaphors with them; and as the original meanings of those metaphors were gradually lost, new stories were invented in order to explain figures no longer recognized as figures of speech. Mythology is therefore 'a disease of language': 'most of the . . . heathen gods are nothing but poetical names, which were gradually allowed to assume a divine personality never contemplated by their original inventors' (1880, p. 12). Comparative philologists are uniquely qualified to eliminate the inherited confusions abounding in a 'late' mythology like that of the Greeks, for they alone know how to reconstruct the root-meanings of all those names which had once denoted natures but which by Homer's time had become largely opaque labels. Daphne's metamorphosis into a laurel when pursued by Apollo is a typical mutation wrought by linguistic disease: behind Daphne stands the Sanskrit Dahana or Ahana, which is the dawn; and as Apollo is the sun, the myth originally described the conflagration of the dawn in the arms of her lover, the sun. As for the laurel? 'The dawn was called δάφνη, the burning; so was the laurel, as wood that burns easily' (1881, p. 399). In fact, a good deal of Greek mythology centres on dawns and sunsets in Müller's far-fetched readings: 'another magnificent sunset looms in the myth of the death of Herakles', he notes with evident satisfaction (1881, p. 394). Disbelievers mocked his reductiveness more easily than his philology in spoofs of his methods. E. B. Tylor proved 'A Song of Sixpence' to be a hitherto unnoticed solar myth; and among unsuspected solar deities currently at large in England, Andrew Lang evidenced W. E. Gladstone, and R. F. Littledale, Müller himself. But there is more to Müller than this. His emphasis on the verbality of mythology, however absurd in practice, was a salutary reminder that myths may be inspired as much by words as ideas; and indeed, Stéphane Mallarmé and the French Symbolists were soon to assert the primacy of word over idea in the creation of poetry, where the words themselves open up possibilities undreamed of in a pre-verbal state. If we agree with Wittgenstein that philosophy is a battle against the bewitchment of our intelligence by words, we may well conclude that mythology is often a condition of willing bewitchment, and assent to John Crowe

Ransom's view that 'myths are conceits, born of metaphor' (*The World's Body* [New York, 1938], p. 140).

Myths and rituals

If it is not the word which was in the beginning, then is it the thought, or the deed? When E. B. Tylor took up this problem in a wide-ranging book on *Primitive Culture* (London, 1871), he conceded Müller's point about the versatility of mythological elaboration but insisted that myths arose originally in primitive man's illogical outlook on the world about him. 'I take material myth to be the primary, and verbal myth to be the secondary formation', he wrote (1873, vol. i, p. 299): in the beginning was the thought, and the thought was analogical. Suppose, however, that Goethe's Faust is right after all: can we evade that old and insoluble problem of the priority of words and thoughts by giving priority to the deed? The possibility was opened up in Robertson Smith's book on *The Religion of the Semites* (Edinburgh, 1889), which investigates the relationship between religious ritual and dogma. 'In all antique religions,' Smith notes, 'mythology takes the place of dogma', but 'this mythology was no essential part of ancient religion, for it had no sacred sanction and no binding-force on the worshippers' (1889, p. 18f.). If that is the case, neither the verbality nor the thought-content of a myth is particularly important, for all it does is to record a pre-existent ritual act. 'So far as myths consist of explanations of ritual their value is altogether secondary, and it may be affirmed with confidence that in almost every case the myth was derived from the ritual, and not the ritual from the myth' (1889, p. 19). If biblical rituals are the source of biblical mythology, perhaps we should look for the ultimate origin of myth in primordial ritual; in which case there is no better place to start than amongst the materials assembled in the twelve volumes of J. G. Frazer's

The Golden Bough (London, 1890–1915), dedicated to Robertson Smith in gratitude and admiration.

Now that anthropologists take the trouble (it is really no trouble at all) to show us that *The Golden Bough* is little more than a gilded twig – its irredeemably Ruskinian style concealing deficiencies of argument and interpretation – Frazer's great work is consolidating its reputation as 'the major informing presence and tutelary genius for the modern mythopoeic imagination' (Vickery, 1972, p. xii), and is therefore being relieved of the strain imposed by an obligation to be factually accurate. What the non-specialist knows about ritual practices derives largely from Frazer and his disciples, whose accounts of love and death in a primitive state make such matters seem enviably important, enviably dignified. How pleasant to make love in the fields knowing that one is ensuring their fertility by an act of methectic insemination; how splendid to experience neither guilt nor fear of punishment when murdering a king in his prime lest the circumjacent world degenerate sympathetically in his old age. How simple and satisfying to find everything modelled on the seasonal shift from spring to winter, and from winter to spring; from birth to death, and from death to rebirth and renewal. So despite the fact that Frazer became more of a euhemerist than a ritualist in the course of his enquiries, *The Golden Bough* provides enough documentation to convince an apperceptive reader that primitive man is deeply preoccupied with the rites of spring, and that some sort of vegetation-ritual was the central activity from which all mythologies subsequently derived. And when Arnold van Gennep published his study of puberty ceremonies, *Les Rites de Passage* (Paris, 1909), the vegetation-pattern of birth, death and rebirth was shown to be mimed in human terms in the rituals by which children undergo symbolic deaths before being reborn as adults.

Hyman (1958) has traced the extraordinarily wide dissemination of the ritual hypothesis after Jane Harrison developed it so eruditely in *Themis* (Cambridge, 1912), a book which sets out to show that the verbal similarity between *drama* and *dromenon* (rite) is by no means accidental. Here it was that Gilbert Murray first displayed his celebrated mock-up of the transitional form between ritual and tragedy, a form still fossilized in the *Bacchae* of Euripides. The only part of this fascinating story which concerns us here is the resultant and unfortunate designation of myth as the poor relation of ritual. Rites, according to Harrison, consist of 'the thing *done*, the δρώμενον proper' and 'the thing *said*, τὸ λεγόμενον' (1912, p. 42). 'A *mythos* to the Greeks was primarily just a thing spoken, uttered by the *mouth*' and therefore merely 'the spoken correlative of the acted rite, the thing done' (1912, p. 328). Nothing more? Judicious assessments by Kluckhohn (1942) and Fontenrose (1971) of the ritual approach to myth indicate various forms of dissent from Harrison. One way of querying the universal priority of ritual is to locate indisputable cases of antecedent myth, as Kluckhohn himself does in citing the Mass as an example of a ritual based upon a sacred story. Alternatively, Harrison's definition of myth may be found inadequate. Fontenrose, for instance, suspects that the *mythoi* she talks about are really verbal formulae and not myths in the narrative sense at all (1971, p. 53); Kirk believes she was misled by eliminating from her definition of myth those very elements which separate it from ritual, such as fantasy, and the freedom to develop (1970, p. 25). When a diligent search for anomalies produces evidence of serious disjunction – rituals unchaperoned by myths, and vice-versa – ritualists prefer to modify their case rather than withdraw it; myth ceases to be proclaimed the child of ritual, and both become siblings of the same parent. Harrison herself made such an adjustment. An early enthusiasm for the aesthetics of Roger Fry refined her conviction that both art and ritual originate in 'unsatisfied desire' (1913, pp. 26, 41); and by the time *Epilegomena to the Study of Greek Religion* was published, she had come to believe that 'mythology . . . springs like ritual from arrested, unsatisfied desire' (1921, p. 27f.). The moderate position, therefore, is to believe that myth and ritual 'replicate each other; the myth exists on the conceptual level and the ritual on the level of action' (Lévi-Strauss, 1963, p. 232). What starts out emotionally from Harrison's 'unsatisfied desire' or intellectually from the Herskovits' 'antecedent idea' (1958, p. 107) is believed generally to end up dramatized as a rite or narrated as a myth. This has proved a particularly attractive theory to a number of writers and so-called 'myth-critics', some of whom are mentioned in chapter four below. 'You have no idea how much I got out of that *Ritual and Art* book', D. H. Lawrence told a correspondent in December 1913: 'it *is* a good idea – but a school marmy woman who writes it.' Now that we know something of what Lawrence got out of Jane Harrison's popularization of her theory in *Ancient Art and Ritual* (London, 1913), we can also appreciate why other writers should have had their reservations. For a wordman has much to lose by the dissociation of myth from ritual and the inequalities consequent upon the implied division of labour. 'In poetry the rite is verbal', Auden claims: 'it pays homage by naming' (*The Dyer's Hand* [London, 1963], p. 57). By cultivating that faculty of divine onomatheia by which Adam named the animals, and named them correctly, a poet may hope to heal the split between word and deed, and by re-integrating myth with ritual evade the odium of a false choice.

Structuralist approaches

The structuralist technique for analysing myth developed from a seminal distinction made in Ferdinand de Saussure's *Cours de Linguistique Générale* (Genève, 1916) between diachronic and synchronic approaches to language-study. The more familiar of the pair is the diachronic or historical approach, which implies that any moment in time can be broken down into constituent elements, each of which is fully intelligible only in terms of its own individual past. Time takes on the appearance of a telephone-cable, the wires all bundled together but separately connected to different points in the distant past. The synchronic approach, on the other hand, ignores the private histories of individual elements and focuses instead on the relationship between those elements at any particular moment. Instead of peeling individual wires off the telephone-cable of time, you cut a cross-section through it and inspect the pattern made by the severed ends. Synchronics is like chess, said Saussure: you can come in at any point of the game and understand the state of play perfectly; it is not necessary to know where individual pieces stood before you arrived, because the important thing is where they stand now in relation to one another.

Looked at synchronically, no single element of language ever exists in isolation because its identity is determined by the company it keeps, and it maintains that identity by standing in opposition to neighbouring elements. The redefinition of phonology in a manner suggested by Saussure enabled the diachronic study of phonetics to part company from the synchronic study of phonemics. And in terms of this linguistic distinction between phon*etics* and phon*emics*, Kenneth L. Pike (1954) was able to propose a classification system for all fields of enquiry based on the fundamental differences between 'etic' (or diachronic) and 'emic' (or synchronic) approaches. The results are nowadays visible everywhere. The importance of establishing etic 'unit-ideas' in the diachronic history-of-ideas pioneered by Arthur O. Lovejoy is now challenged by Michel Foucault's *archéologie du savoir*, which is grounded on the identification of synchronic *epistèmes*. Alan Dundes advises folklorists to look beyond diachronic motifs in the search for synchronic 'motifemes'; Eugene Dorfman searches for 'narremes' in the *Chanson de Roland* and *Poema del Cid*, and Claude Lévi-Strauss for 'mythemes' in the mythologies of South American Indians.

Non-structuralist approaches to Old Testament myths are frequently comparative and involve atomizing (say) the book of Genesis into etic units which can be paralleled in other cultures. Scholars who read the Garden of Eden story as a Hebrew variant of the Earthly Paradise *topos* are not obliged in their pursuit of analogues to take more than a passing interest in the researches of others who are studying the Genesis account of Creation in the context of universal cosmogonies. A structuralist, however, will insist on treating both the Creation myth and the Eden myth as emic units of that totality we call Genesis, aiming to identify the homologue of Genesis-as-a-whole instead of amassing analogues to discrete parts of it and ending up with a vast, etic *collage* like *The Golden Bough*. 'The true constituent units of a myth', warns Lévi-Strauss, 'are not the isolated relations but *bundles of such relations*, and it is only as bundles that these relations can be put to use and combined so as to produce a meaning' (1963, p. 211). No matter how arbitrary and contrived the constituent elements of Genesis may be in the opinion of textual scholars (and Lévi-Strauss is more inhibited by such considerations than Edmund Leach), our present text of Genesis constitutes a structural whole; and the alleged meaning of that whole may come as a surprise to those who are accustomed to extract meanings from etically selected parts instead of from emically constructed wholes. So when Leach looks at Genesis in a way Lévi-Strauss himself prefers not to, he shows how it can be broken down into sets of binary oppositions, each having its own mediatory category: just as the sky mediates between the waters above the firmament and those below it, so Eve mediates as Adam's helpmeet between man and beast. By dissolving the content of separate stories in order to reveal skeletal patterns of this order, a structuralist may discover that his mythemes exceed their descriptive function by engendering interpretative possibilities which are not accessible to readers who concentrate on narrative sequences. Is the Genesis serpent female, for instance, as misogynous interpreters of the Bible long believed, or phallic in a Freudian way? Apparently neither, for if the serpent mediates between Adam and Eve, as Leach says it does, the odds are that the serpent is hermaphroditic; the Bible, alas, is non-committal.

Leach's analyses of Hebrew and Greek myths are especially courageous in view of a widespread suspicion (stemming originally from Paul Ricoeur) that a structuralist will get far better results from examining the totemic myths of primitive tribes than from the more 'civilized' mythologies of Semitic and Hellenic peoples. Lévi-Strauss is so very plausible when analyzing the Amerindian tale of Asdiwal that it is a pity one of his poorer performances – the Oedipus myth interpreted as a query concerning the allegedly autochthonous origins of man – should be so conspicuously on show as a blackboard example of structuralist methods (1963, pp. 213–17). A sympathetic classicist like Kirk finds it an embarrassment, and it is easy to see why, for morsels of the raw evidence taste distinctly cooked. To equate 'Cadmos kills the Dragon' with 'Oedipus kills the Sphinx' invites Leach's objection that the Sphinx commits suicide. Yet when, in another context, Leach says that Orpheus rescues Eurydice from Hades 'by means of music, but loses her because of silence' (1970, p. 68), it seems perverse of him not to admit that Orpheus loses her because he breaks the taboo forbidding him to look back at her until they have left Hades. No wonder Leach finds the Orpheus myth 'heavily laden with binary antitheses' if this is how they are manufactured. Kirk, on the other hand, is attracted by such methods but critical of their limitations. A confessed revisionist, he sometimes works the other way round from Lévi-Strauss, first establishing his median and then looking outwards for the polarities it mediates. Composite beasts like centaurs or satyrs undoubtedly mediate contrary claims; so too does Pandora, whom Hesiod calls 'a beautiful evil' (*Theogony*, 585). Here and there, as in the story of the Cyclops, Kirk is able to glimpse, through the murk of editorial remodellings, a clear Lévi-Straussian opposition between Nature and Culture.

Somewhat disturbing is the hermeneutical circularity of structuralist analysis, in so far as the tacit messages Lévi-Strauss reveals in myths appear to be constituted by the binary hypothesis he projects in order to explain them. 'The purpose of a myth', he writes, 'is to provide a logical model capable of overcoming a contradiction' (1963, p. 229), perhaps in the way that *Paradise Lost* tries to reconcile predestination with free will. Yet if we set out with the assumption that myths attempt to mediate contradictions in human experience, inevitably we shall find ourselves categorizing the data of myths in terms of statements, counterstatements and compromises: virginity, motherhood and virgin mothers; male, female and hermaphrodite. The logic of Lévi-Strauss's *mythologiques* is basically the pseudo-Hegelian triad of thesis, antithesis and synthesis; and while Leach may assure us that 'binary oppositions are intrinsic to the process of human thought' (1969, p. 9), it has yet to be proved that they are as characteristic of non-European as they are of European thought-processes.

It came as a surprise when Lévi-Strauss collaborated with Roman Jakobson in a study of Baudelaire's sonnet 'Cats', for previously he had distinguished rather sharply between untranslatable poetry and translatable myth (1963, p. 210). But here was Baudelaire with a poem actually inviting structuralist analysis, with a binary opposition in its very first line between fervent lovers and austere scholars (we have it on Yeats' authority that young men tossing on their beds are totally unlike scholars who cough in ink) and a sphinx-like cat which obligingly mediates a *coincidentia oppositorum*. Given this much encouragement, he and Jakobson dismantle and reassemble the poem several times over, stacking the parts in a variety of orders. What distinguishes their reading of Baudelaire from ours is their ingenious demonstration (over-ingenious, Riffaterre would say) that the visible macro-structure of the poem is repeated unconsciously time after time in the microstructure of rhyme-schemes, syntax, gender and so on. This is the 'mythic' dimension of the poem, as Lévi-Strauss understands it, for 'the function of repetition is to render the structure of the myth apparent' (1963, p. 229). This time, however, emic analysis yields no surprises. Jakobson and Lévi-Strauss tell us only what we knew already but tell it in far more detail than we ever suspected, or than we really need. If Baudelaire did indeed create unconsciously in his sonnet a set of microstructures which we, his readers, are equally unconscious of, then in what sense can they be said to exist? Structuralism has the distinction of supplying a purely analytic explanation of myth which differs from all the others here considered in opening up no new dimension whatsoever to the practising writer, whose continuing fascination with mythology is our next concern.

3

Myths and writers

Mythology as heritage

'Fable is the patrimony of the arts', wrote Nicolas Fréret; 'it is an inexhaustible source of ingenious ideas, pleasing images, interesting subjects, allegories, and emblems' (Feldman & Richardson, 1972, p. 96). As such, it has something to offer everybody. It not only provides ready-made Brillo boxes for poetasters to scribble their names on, but also encourages more talented *bricoleurs* like Spenser or Jonson to build entirely new structures from bits and pieces salvaged from widely disparate myths. While moralists see pride coming before a fall in the story of Phaeton, sensualists contribute lubricious details to descriptions of Pygmalion's statue, and invent those erotic-mythological narrative poems we now call *epyllia*, of which Marlowe's *Hero and Leander* and Shakespeare's *Venus and Adonis* are the best known examples (Donno). *Fay ce que vouldras* (Do what thou wilt) is the Rabelaisian motto. You are free to invent your own myths along the lines of those found in Ovid, as Marlowe does when having his heroine courted by Apollo in *Hero and Leander* (1593); or you can pretend to set the record straight by 'correcting' some well-known myth, as in William Browne's conceit that Narcissus pined to death after looking at the face of some other beautiful boy (*Britannia's Pastorals*, i[1613], ii, ll. 411ff.). You display your originality by exercising ingenuity in discovering new ways of writing about old myths. Operating within a network of shared allusions among educated readers, you can by-pass the explicit in order to explore the tacit and ironic. Milton's unfallen Eve re-enacts the self-infatuation of Narcissus before a pool, although Narcissus' name is never mentioned (*Paradise Lost*, iv. 460ff.); and when she is compared fleetingly to Pandora (iv. 714), we ourselves draw the correct and ominous conclusion. Or at least, that is what it all used to be like, once upon a time.

Although major writers like Spenser and Milton were immensely learned, the writing and reading of mythological literature was not nearly so exacting as it might appear. In addition to the famous translations of Ovid by Arthur Golding (1565–7) and George Sandys (1632), and of Homer by George Chapman (1611–15), there were numerous mythological handbooks supplying short-cuts to erudition: Boccaccio's *De Genealogia Deorum* (Venice, 1472), Lilio Giraldi's *De Deis Gentium* (Basel, 1548), Natale Conti's *Mythologiae* (Venice, 1567), and Vincenzo Cartari's *Le Imagini colla Sposizione degli Dei degli Antichi* (Venice, 1556), which was abridged and Englished by Robert Lynche as *The Fountain of Ancient Fiction* (London, 1599). A surly comment in the early fifteenth-century *Siege of Thebes* by John Lydgate reveals an uneasy attitude towards such undoubtedly useful books which pre-empt the writer's task:

> Of Lycurgus you get no more of me.
> But the truth if you list verify
> Read *Of Gods the Genealogy* ...   (11. 3536ff.)

And two-and-a-half centuries later Robert Lloyd was still mocking 'The Poetry Professors' for their slavish dependence on mythological manuals by 'Fabricius, Cooper, Calepine/ Ainsworthius, Faber, Constantine' (*Poetical Works* [London, 1774], i, 36). John Marston made the point in 1598 that an obscure poem put together with the aid of Conti or Cartari is most easily unfathomed by reference to their books ('Satire ii') – which is precisely what scholars like Gombrich and Seznec have done in disentangling some of the complex webs of Renaissance art and literature. Yet the influence of mythological manuals on writers and artists, however probable, is difficult to prove, for nobody ever acknowledges borrowings from such works (Steadman, 1972, p. 27). Starnes and Talbert have tried to establish that even the lexicons used in schools (such as the *Dictionarium Historicum ac Poeticum* [Paris, 1553] by Charles Estienne [Stephanus], or Thomas Cooper's *Thesaurus Linguae Romanae & Britannicae* [London, 1565]) contributed both to the phrasing and content of major Renaissance poems and plays. Their valuable book displays the usual short-comings of source-studies; and while it is sensible of them to look for sources in handbooks everybody consulted regularly, even the striking parallels they adduce remain inconclusive on account of the commonplace nature of the material. If 'E.K.' appears to quote Cooper verbatim when referring to Flora, the goddess of flowers, as a famous harlot, we have to remember that *Flora meretrix* figures prominently also in Boccaccio's book on famous women, as well as in other mythological handbooks of the period (Held, 1961, p. 210). But it is certainly surprising to learn that nearly every detail in Jonson's seemingly erudite *Masque of Augurs* (1621–2) was easily available in such works.

In the heyday of Renaissance mythomania, immediacy was much prized. Even though Jonson might attempt a historical reconstruction of Roman marriage customs in *Hymenaei* (1606), and Landor later aspire to write Hellenics (1846) which were supposed to look as though they had been written by an ancient Greek, the consensus of opinion favoured quite the opposite procedure. Good writers aimed at domiciling classical mythology so successfully that it would blend into an English setting as easily as the dryads and fauns flit through Jonson's poem 'To Penshurst'. Anachronisms helped create the illusion that myths are not just tales retold but realities lived: Hero's fan, and the gloves she never wears, help transport Marlowe's epyllion from the lost worlds of Musaeus and Ovid into an Elizabethan here and now. A chasm separates Chaucer's

medievalizing of classical materials in *Troilus and Creseyde*
(which in its time was 'modern') from the medievalizing in
William Morris' *The Story of Orpheus and Eurydice* (1865–70),
which was quaint to begin with. In its political aspect, immediacy means relevance. The obliquities of *Samson Agonistes*
(1671) make Milton's play as much a commentary on the Civil
War and its aftermath as an embellishment of the Book of
Judges; and the matter of Troy took on a fresh significance
during that low, dishonest decade in which Jean Giraudoux
wrote *La Guerre de Troie n'Aura pas Lieu* (1935). Myths are
malleable. What T. S. Eliot does with the myth of Orestes in
The Family Reunion (1939) is very different from what Jean-
Paul Sartre does with it in *Les Mouches* (1943), but there is no
point in trying to decide which of them has the more correct
view of Orestes. Change – in the form of creative misunder-
standings – is what keeps myths alive. Even something as radi-
cally iconotropic as D. H. Lawrence's *Apocalypse* (London,
1932), which transvaluates the Revelation of St John by making
a life-assertive dragon out of the Beast with Seven Heads, has
the virtue of re-mythifying basic materials in the very process
of up-ending them. Myths can tolerate almost any kind of
treatment except indifference or the solicitousness of historical
scholarship; for as soon as a passion for accuracy sets in and
people begin to point out 'mistakes' or 'medieval impurities'
in (say) Spenser's mythology, the literary scene is very soon
cluttered with what Bush calls 'plaster reproductions of the
antique' (1937, p. 529). Calculated indifference, of course, is
more immediately and efficiently corrosive.

Enlightenment and demythologizing

Every so often attempts are made to eradicate mythology on
the grounds that we would be much better off without it.
Whenever such an Enlightenment occurs, myths are held to be
rather childish, certainly passé, and quite untrue. Let us take
the last accusation first.

We can read in Thomas Sprat's *History of the Royal Society* (London, 1667) how classical mythology came to be degraded as the natural sciences gained prestige in the seventeenth century. 'The wit of the fables and religions of the ancient world is well-nigh consumed', Sprat writes. 'They have already served the poets long enough, and it is high time to dismiss them' (p. 413). It is not the ornamental aspect of classical mythology which worries Sprat, but the fact that it perpetuates falsehoods. Sprat counters the Shakespearian argument that the truest poetry is the most feigning by asserting that 'truth is never so well expressed or amplified as by those ornaments which are true and real in themselves'; and he hopes that writers will in future collaborate in the Enlightenment endeavour by restricting their activities to the embellishment of verifiable truths (which, incidentally, will ensure that their writings will not suffer the fate of the Ancients' in being rendered obsolete by scientific enquiry). This sophistical appeal to reason was strengthened at the time by an equally disingenuous appeal to common experience, which confirmed that no modern writer had ever seen a Celtic fairy, let alone a Grecian goddess; for the nymphs had long ago departed, and left no addresses. Fairies had last been plentiful in the days of Mary Tudor, wrote Richard Corbet in 'The Fairies' Farewell':

> But, since of late Elizabeth,
> And later, James came in,
> They never danced on any heath
> As when the time hath been.

Hobbesian rationalists of a Protestant persuasion might rejoice that the march of mind had eliminated such superstitious nonsense, but conservationists could only mourn a vanished species. 'There are no Dryads in Hyde Park', remarks Peacock, 'nor Naiads in the Regent's Canal' (*The Four Ages of Poetry*, 1819). With wild Nature either method-

ized by landscape-gardeners or tamed by industrial entre-
preneurs, the old gods had nowhere to go. No self-respecting
deity could live in a wood 'where the only inscription is not
Genio loci, but "Trespassers will be prosecuted",' complains
Mr Falconer in Peacock's novel, *Gryll Grange* (1861, ch. 9):
'there can be . . . no Naiad in a stream that turns a cotton-mill;
no Oread in a mountain dell, where a railway train deposits a
cargo of Vandals; no Nereids or Oceanitides along the sea-
shore, where a coastguard is watching for smugglers.' A more
thoughtful Karl Marx moved beyond mere outrage at such
scenes to note how all imaginative creations are made redundant by technological innovations: what other conclusion
was to be drawn from the fact that Jupiter's thunderbolt is
rendered harmless by the lightning-conductor, and the
quicksilver Hermes ineluctably trapped by the *Crédit mobilier*
(*Critique of Political Economy*, 1857 draft, section 4)?

Those who disparaged the truth-claims of pagan mythology
could generally depend on Christian support, for the Church
had always insisted that a pagan, no matter how intelligent, is
by definition denied the light of Christian revelation and so can
never acquire those insights which are conferred only by
divine grace. The proximity of 'verifiable' truth (in Sprat's
sense) to 'revealed' truth (in the Christian sense) comes out
very clearly in the words with which an admirer of Royal
Society procedures, Abraham Cowley, prefaces his *Davideis*
(1668): he prays to God

> T'unbind the charms that in slight fables lie,
> And teach that Truth is truest poesy.

The *Davideis* was part of an ambitious and widespread effort
to prove that a modern literature based on the Bible, which
is true, has a good chance of overgoing ancient literatures
based on pagan mythologies, which are false. Milton could
feel confident that the very subject-matter of *Paradise Lost*
was 'not less but more heroic' (ix. 14) than that of the *Iliad*

or the *Aeneid*; and Joseph Beaumont hoped that his daunting poem on the intercourse betwixt Christ and the Soul, *Psyche* (1648), would show 'that a divine theme is as capable and happy a subject of poetical ornament, as any pagan or human device whatsoever.' A programme for such performances had developed in an earlier fashion for sacred parodies (like George Herbert's 'Jordan' poems) which permit the retention of classical rhetoric but not of classical ornament, thus challenging writers to find Biblical approximations to the fauna and flora of classical locations. Some anonymous verses in commendation of Edward Benlowes' *Theophila* (1652) state the *contrafactum* credo baldly and unequivocally:

> A hallowed poet's Muse is th' Holy Dove.
> Parnassus th' empyrean height above.
> His lofty-soaring Pegasus Christ's love.
> Heaven's shower of Grace is his Castalian spring.

Deucalion is easily replaceable by Noah in such an aesthetic, as is Hercules by Samson. 'Can all the transformations of the gods', asks Cowley, 'give such copious hints to flourish and expatiate on, as the true miracles of Christ, or of his prophets and apostles?' (preface to *Works*, 1668). So it came about that science and religion joined in uneasy truce to denounce the falsehood of pagan mythology.

Another point commonly stressed in Enlightenment criticism is that whatever literary potential mythology once possessed has now been exhausted through over-exploitation: classical mythology, Coleridge was to conclude, is 'an exploded mythology' (*Biographia Literaria* [London, 1817], ch. 18). Ironically, the educational system which familiarized readers with the mythological knowledge upon which classical literacy depends, had the adverse effect of over-familiarizing selected myths and eroding them into clichés. Writers and readers were alike sensitive to the problem. People engaged in the never-ending business of modernizing literature must inevitably come to regard the 'myth-kitty' (Philip Larkin's term) as unnecessary luggage: ignoring it becomes a virtue. Thomas Carew, in his great elegy on the Dean of St Paul's (1633), applauds Donne's abstemiousness in not dipping into Ovid's *Metamorphoses* or getting the 'penurious, bankrupt age' in which he lived any more deeply in debt to the Ancients. The banking metaphor turns up again as Walt Whitman envisages a new-world poetry devoid of old-world mythologies ('Song of the Exposition', ii):

> Come Muse migrate from Greece and Ionia,
> Cross out please those immensely overpaid accounts,
> That matter of Troy and Achilles' wrath, and Aeneas',
>   Odysseus' wanderings,
> Placard 'Removed' and 'To Let' on the rocks of your
>   snowy Parnassus . . .
> For know a better, fresher, busier sphere, a wide,
>   untried domain awaits, demands you.

Rupert Brooke would have said it was easier for Whitman than for an English poet to try to get along without using classical mythology because Whitman had the advantage of living in that godforsaken place, America, where 'the maple and the birch conceal no dryads, and Pan has never been heard amongst [the] reed-beds' (*Letters from America* [London, 1916], p. 155).

Wordsworth published an illuminating note on his 'Ode to Lycoris' (1817) in which he explains how 'the hackneyed and lifeless use into which mythology fell towards the close of the seventeenth century' inhibited him from introducing classical allusions into his earliest poetry (this, I suppose, would be his answer to the accusation Byron makes in *Don Juan* [iii, 99] that the reason why Wordsworth made no reference to Charles' Wain or Medea's dragon in *The Waggoners* is that such references were 'too classic for his vulgar brain'). But now, in 1817, Wordsworth feels that the situation is once more changing for the better, so much so that the old mythology, if allied to 'real sentiment', has become viable again. Jaded readers confirmed the writers' fears that mythological themes had grown irredeemably stale by the eighteenth century. 'The attention naturally retires from a new tale of Venus, Diana, and Minerva', Johnson confessed when writing about John Gay in *The Lives of the Poets* (London, 1781), and revealed in his criticism of Nicholas Rowe's *Ulysses* (1706) that the Augustan dissatisfaction with classical mythology was abetted by an inflexible conservatism which eliminated the only possible remedy. 'We have been too early acquainted with the poetical heroes', he writes, 'to expect any pleasure from their revival: to show them as they have already been shown is to disgust by repetition; to give them new qualities or new adventures is to offend by violating received notions.' Mythology, in short, is a bore, but it would be indecorous to try to make it less boring. This is one of the reasons why Addison was driven to publish a mock-edict forbidding the modern poet to invoke any god or goddess (*Spectator*, 30 October 1712). Because a poem 'should carry in it all the colours of truth', writers should eschew pagan falsities and remember that 'nothing can be more ridiculous than to have recourse to our Jupiters and Junos.' Authoresses are exempted from Addison's edict, as they generally do exactly as they please anyway; so too are school-boys, who may use the myths in five-finger exercises while learning the art of composition. But when one becomes a man, one is expected to put aside such childish toys, for to play with pagan mythology is 'unpardonable in a poet that is past sixteen'.

Addison's denigration of myth as childish typifies the Enlightenment attitude, for the rational mind characteristically confers maturity upon its own workings and finds varying degrees of immaturity in alternative mental habits. Myth is believed to serve no useful purpose except to the intellectually handicapped, who will never make the Cartesian grade. Spinoza, for example, was never in any doubt that Hebrew mythology had been invented for 'the masses whose intellect is not capable of perceiving things clearly and distinctly' (*Tractatus Theologico-Politicus* [1670], ch. 5). In the progressivist scheme of things, history is the evolutionary record of largely unsuccessful attempts to achieve rational perfection, the human life-span providing a conceptual model for the process. There is no shortage of schemes distinguishing three phases in the evolution of Enlightenment consciousness, and invariably the first phase is the Age of Myth or Fable, which is set way back in the 'childhood' of the human race, before people had learned to think conceptually and express themselves analytically. The tripartite scheme Frazer opts for in *The Golden Bough* (1890–1915) is an evolutionary sequence beginning with an era of Magic and passing through a period of Religion to a final age of Science; and it was left to Freud to synthesize this Frazerian scheme of cultural evolution with his own theory of the way in which individual personality develops. The results were published in *Totem and Taboo* (1913). Here we are offered a comprehensive psycho-cultural theory of human evolution which is a masterpiece of Enlightenment propaganda. Each era in Frazer's scheme entails a corresponding world-view or *Weltanschauung*, which Freud then equates with certain phases in the development of the libido, one of them invented specially for the occasion. The results are best shown diagrammatically.

Phase	Weltanschauung (Frazer)	Libidinal Stage (Freud)	Human Age
1	animistic/ mythological	narcissism	infancy
2	religious	first object-choice (parent)	childhood
3	scientific	second object-choice (external reality)	maturity

Psychologically, neurotics never get beyond the pleasure principle, and therefore never confront reality at phase three; culturally, neither do 'savages' (Frazer and Freud apply this term habitually to all primitive peoples, and quite without embarrassment). The myth-making faculty is truly infantile, as indeed savages are, in the eyes of paternalistic imperialists. And the presence of a myth-making faculty in twentieth-century man is to be interpreted either as an archaic vestige from some aboriginal phase of human consciousness, or as evidence of arrested psychological development. Modern artists are either primitives (some of them are even known as Primitives) or neurotics (Surrealists like Dali came to accept that label too); mature people, of course, should try to be neither. Among the many hidden assumptions in this area of speculation is the now discredited biological theory of re-capitulation which evolutionists took from Ernst Haeckel, and which literary students usually encounter in embryonic form in Sir Thomas Browne's *Religio Medici* (1643, i. 34). According to the theory of recapitulation, the development of a human foetus from conception to birth recapitulates various stages in the evolution of *homo sapiens*: briefly, ontogeny recapitulates phylogeny. 'Something occurred in the life of the human species', Freud was later to write in *Moses and Monotheism* (1939), 'similar to what occurs in the life of individuals' (*CPW*, vol. xxiii, p. 80). Being a product of recapitulatory processes, modern man might easily regress into the savagery from which he has so recently emerged, unless he takes care to avoid ancestral patterns of behaviour. A modern writer who cultivates mythic consciousness is in these terms a sort of evolutionary throwback, a living fossil, perhaps even (in the opinion of that hysterical reactionary, Max Nordau) a psychopathological degenerate. It is not hard to imagine what Nordau (or Freud, for that matter) would have thought of Thomas Mann's exploration of the recapitulatory paradox that whereas 'in the life of the human race the mythical is an early and primitive stage, in the life of the individual it is a late and mature one' (*Essays of Three Decades* [London, 1947], p. 422). Mann here comes close to the anti-Freudian position taken by Jung, who believed that myths are 'the most mature product of young humanity' (*CW*, vol. v, p. 24). When writers come to realize that they must not expect to grow away from myth, but grow towards it, Romanticism triumphs, and the child once more becomes father to the man. In Friedrich Nietzsche's evocation of the Dionysiac origins of Greek tragedy we can see Enlightenment contempt for the primitive transformed into Romantic admiration. *The Birth of Tragedy* (1872) treats Socratic man as an evolutionary mistake; and when this happens, the poet's mythopoeic powers are bound to appear a truly miraculous survival for which we should be very grateful indeed.

There is a tenacious belief that myth is closely, if obscurely, connected with literature; so much so that the fate of one is bound up with that of the other, thus engendering fears for the future of literature whenever a spell of demythologizing sets in. 'Mythology and poetry are one and inseparable', wrote Schlegel (1800, p. 82); and if we find ourselves agreeing with him it is largely because Europeans tend to think of mythology as an exclusively Greco-Roman phenomenon, without always realizing that Greco-Roman mythology is preserved in a highly sophisticated literary form. Folklorists point out that what we find in Euripides or Ovid is not really mythology but rather literature made out of myths, literature made by craftsmen who tamper artfully with myths so as to create something which, in its stabilized and codified form, is quite remote from what the anthropologist encounters in his fieldwork. To tell a folklorist that myths are important largely because they are the raw material of literature is like telling a literary critic that novels are important as the raw materials of films. Literary people have a habit of looking upon the most artistically wrought version of a myth as being somehow typical of mythology at its best, and of disparaging anything else as mere barbarism; so they do not take kindly to investigators who probe the pre-literary origins of myth and come up with such revelations as that Penelope was originally a purple-striped duck (Farnell, 1919, p. 41). Instead, myths are held to be like works of literature by virtue of being works of imagination, anonymous and collectivist admittedly, but no less imaginative for all that. 'The greatest piece of fiction: Greek mythology': so runs the adage of a connoisseur of supreme fiction, Wallace Stevens. Advocates of this view usually point out that metaphor is structurally the common ground between myth and literature, although they may differ on the question of genesis. Is a metaphor a condensed myth, or is a myth an inflated metaphor? Vico was inclined to think that 'every metaphor . . . is a fable in brief' (*Scienza Nuova* [1725–44], p. 116), which accords with Emerson's view of language as 'fossil poetry' ('The Poet', 1844), every word of which turns out to be a 'petrified poem' when inspected by Max Müller (*Biographies of Words* [London, 1888], p. x). Others, like Otto Rank (*Art and Artist* [New York, 1932], pp. 207–31), regard myths as the product of metaphors which have been taken in a literal sense – 'conceits born of metaphors', as Ransom puts it (see above, p. 35). And there are those, like Northrop Frye, who take from Aristotle their definition of myth as plot, and proceed on the assumption that 'myth is a structural element in literature because literature as a whole is a "displaced" mythology' (1963, p. 1). None of them questions the basic affinity between myth and literature, although few would accept unreservedly those spurious stemmata one sometimes encounters which trace the successive 'displacements' by means of which myth became literature through intermediary forms like legends, fairy-tales, folktales, ballads and so forth.

While formalists seek the origins of myth in metaphor, affectivists (who believe that the way people react to something is a sure guide to its nature) try to bridge the gap between myth and literature by arguing that both are alike in possessing the same spell-binding powers. Here we usually encounter a fair amount of legerdemain with that nebulous term *mana*, which R. H. Codrington introduced in his book on *The Melanesians* (Oxford, 1891), and which seems to imply belief in a supernatural efficaciousness resident in some thereby privileged object or person (Capell). Chase reports that 'myth is literature which suffuses the natural with preternatural efficacy' (1949, p. 78); Holloway finds in *mana* 'the idea of the imaginative work as a source of power (an idea confirmed . . . by the work's effects)' (1960, p. 127). Loosely used in myth-criticism, *mana* is an honorific term appended to selected books as a signalling-device to people who cultivate the *mysterium tremendum* and shudder knowledgeably as they read.

Those who emphasize differences between myths and literature generally think in terms of form-and-content categories. 'The myth and the poem differ in this', writes Herbert Read; 'the myth persists by virtue of its *imagery*, and this imagery can be conveyed by means of the verbal symbols of any language . . . . But a poem persists by virtue of its *language*; its essence belongs to that language and cannot be translated' (1938, p. 178). If the same myth can be displayed equally well in a painting as in a poem, there may be grounds for believing with C. S. Lewis that myths are wholly extra-literary, and that 'the value of myth is not a specifically literary value, nor the appreciation of myth a specifically literary experience' (1961, p. 46). To Lewis, the events which myths record are more important than the forms which record them, which is what one might expect a Christian to say in defence of the Gospels. Whereas an anthropologist like Lévi-Strauss quite readily acknowledges that 'the myth consists of all its versions' (1963, p. 217), literary critics are much more fastidious, and do not look upon Goethe's *Faust* (1832) as an optional version of Marlowe's *Tragical History of Doctor Faustus* (1588). A myth is an open-ended process; a work of literature is a closed product. Anybody may contribute his little bit to a myth, but is obliged to respect the original integrity of a poem or play. Failure (or refusal) to grasp this point results in controversies like the one provoked in the 1960s by the Kott-inspired productions of Zeffirelli, who treated Shakespeare's plays as myths instead of texts, and dislodged the scholars' Shakespeare in order to make room for Shakespeare our contemporary.

Nobody has yet proved that literature is or is not myth. Nor has anyone been able to resolve the difference in emphasis between Mark Schorer's 'myth is the indispensable sub-structure of poetry' and Richard Chase's 'poetry is the indispensable substructure of myth' (1949, p. 109). When a critic of Chase's distinction comes to retract (1957) the approach he defended originally at book-length, we may find ourselves drifting towards that compromise position taken by Malinowski when he wrote that 'myth contains germs of the future epic, romance and tragedy' (1926, p. 118). For him as for Vickery (1966, p. ix), myth is 'the matrix out of which literature emerges both historically and psychologically.'

A literature in the process of being demythologized will run for some time on the momentum built up by earlier mytholo-gizers, in so far as what one's immediate forbears have taken at face value will provide rich opportunities for parody, travesty and burlesque. Ovid survived his medieval purgatory as *Ovide Moralisé* only to enter the Enlightenment as *Ovide Bouffon*, which is the title of a book by L. Richer (Paris, 1662), one of many such works inspired by Paul Scarron's *Virgile Travesti* (Paris, 1648). This is the first phase of demythologiz-ing, the phase which supports a mock-heroic masterpiece like Pope's *Rape of the Lock* (1714), and which (for all its super-ficial hostility to myths and their makers) depends heavily upon the existence of a reading-public well-acquainted with classical mythology: 'it is only in an age of faith', Bush reminds us, 'that

a feast of fools can be enjoyed' (1932, p. 293). By the time the
second phase is reached (which is where we are now), the
parodies themselves have become meaningless to a generation
no longer familiar with what is being parodied, and handbooks
are required to explain epic features to readers otherwise
insensitive to mock-heroic niceties. How remote from current
classroom experience is that story Coleridge tells at the beginning of *Biographia Literaria* (1817), of how his own school-
master used to forbid his students to refer to Pegasus or
Parnassus or Hippocrene in their compositions, and would
convert every 'Pierian spring' he encountered into a 'cloister-
pump'. Rare indeed is the writer who can evoke that precarious
moment between belief and disbelief when scepticism articu-
lates itself as elegantly as it does in Andrew Marvell's mytho-
tropic rendering of two celebrated metamorphoses:

> Apollo hunted Daphne so,
> Only that she might laurel grow.
> And Pan did after Syrinx speed,
> Not as a nymph, but for a reed.

Most mythoclasts wield a sledge-hammer. What nonsense, they
will say, to pretend that the story of Hero and Leander is a
tragedy of romantic love: Leander 'went but forth to wash
himself in the Hellespont, and being taken with the cramp was
drowned' (*As You Like It*, IV. i. 103ff.). Euhemerus is the
debunker's vade-mecum: that seemingly scandalous story
about Pasiphae and the bull simply means

> That Pasiphae promoted breeding cattle
> To make the Cretans bloodier in battle.
>
> (*Don Juan*, ii. 155)

And while all this is going on in a comic subplot, as it were, to
the great drama of demythologization, the main plot is taken
up with the business of rationalizing mythology in such a way
that the old pantheon is converted into a sort of alphabet of

personified abstractions, each deity being reduced to a single quality – some clear and distinct philosophical idea – and then frozen eternally in a representative gesture. As the Enlightenment dawns, it is inevitably the fate of gods and goddesses to be humiliated by parody or mummified by prosopopoeia. And it is the fate of mythology as a whole to petrify into those clichés which once formed the staple of middle-brow journalism, where undesirable alternatives are always labelled Scylla and Charybdis, and every weakness is an Achilles' heel.

Or so it would seem. Fortunately, writers have the courage to resist prevailing modes of determinism, and demonstrate time and again that our anxiety over the future of myth in an era of unwaveringly rationalistic scrutiny is ill-founded. Myths can be weakened but hardly annihilated by disbelief; for a successful mythology is one which encourages people to invent new and more reputable reasons for believing in it after the old ones are no longer tenable. We can see something of this process in Chaucer, who was not dissuaded from rewriting Boccaccio's *Teseide* as *The Knight's Tale* simply because he could not credit pagan deities with the powers they were reputed to have. Instead, he 'astrologized' the gods for the benefit of readers who could accept the theory of planetary influences more readily than the existence of those gods after whom the planets were named (Curry). We discover a new value in mythological discards by looking at them in a different way, a way made possible by a new mythogony. One need not read very far into modern literature to realize that a good deal of the mythology one encounters there owes its existence to the new perspectives opened up by Freudian psychology.

It is in debates concerning the demythologization of the Bible that we encounter a fresh perspective on the Enlightenment dilemma as it occurs in literature. Basic differences between Rudolf Bultmann and Karl Jaspers rest on the fact that Bultmann takes an ornamentalist view of myth, whereas

Jaspers opts for an incarnational view. I call Bultmann an ornamentalist because he believes that by stripping the New Testament of its mythic accretions one can encounter that naked *kerygma* which proclaims divine truth. Jaspers, on the other hand, takes the Wordsworthian view that verbal expression is no mere 'dress' of pre-existent 'thought' but the very incarnation of thought, and finds it impossible to dissociate myth from *kerygma* without losing all in the attempt. If the Bultmann-Jaspers debate is reducible in this way to literary-critical terms, it ought to illuminate what happens in Augustan literature; and indeed Sanford Budick has observed how in Dryden's *Absalom and Achitophel* (1681) and Johnson's *The Vanity of Human Wishes* (1749) the 'kerygmatic' dismantling of an old myth invariably heralds the advent of a new one. What a literary critic can learn from Bultmann and Jaspers is the importance of dissociating that kind of debunking which usually goes by the name of 'demythologizing' from what Bultmann calls *Entmythologisierung*, which is not so much a destructive as a decreative endeavour, an attempt to salvage something worth while, a *kerygma*, from those obsolete encrustations which obscure it. However strenuously critics may try to demythologize literature, writers are unlikely to tolerate anything more radical than an *Entmythologisierung*.

Survivals and revivals

Leigh Hunt, writing on 'Fiction and Matter of Fact' in 1824, found it remarkable that people of his generation had become exceedingly fond of 'a new and more primitive use of the old pagan mythology, so long and so mechanically abused by the Chloes and Venuses of the French.' When the world was too much with Wordsworth, he imagined how better off he would be as 'a pagan suckled in a creed outworn', if only to catch a glimpse of 'Proteus rising from the sea;/Or hear old Triton

blow his wreathèd horn' (*Miscellaneous Sonnets*, xxxiii [1807]).
The mentality which could unweave a rainbow prismatically,
or clip an angel's wings, inevitably jeopardized the viewless
wings of poesy in the opinion of John Keats, who voiced his
fear in the preface to *Endymion* (1818) that perhaps he had 'in
too late a day touched the beautiful mythology of Greece'.
Wordsworth, who should have known better, dismissed the
'Hymn to Pan' section of *Endymion* (i. 232–306) as 'a very
pretty piece of paganism'; but to find such things theologically
reprehensible was becoming old-fashioned, and quite beside
the point. 'Heathenism is lovely *because* it is dead', wrote
Francis Thompson in 1888. 'To read Keats is to grow in love
with Paganism; but it is the Paganism of Keats. Pagan
Paganism was not poetical' (*Works* [London, 1913], vol. iii,
p. 39). Romantic neopaganism is an aesthetic rather than a
theological issue, although grounded in a conviction that
Christianity is ultimately life-denying and anti-art. Swinburne
assesses the situation in his 'Hymn to Proserpine' (1866),
echoing the apocryphal dying words of Julian the Apostate
(*Vicisti Galilaee*):

> Thou hast conquered, O pale Galilean; the world
>   has grown grey from thy breath;
> We have drunken of things Lethean, we have fed on
>   the fullness of death.

Opponents of the pale Galilean were not so much atheists as
aesthetes who interpreted the conflict between paganism and
Christianity as basically a conflict between art and morality.
Théophile Gautier makes this explicit in his poem 'Bûchers et
Tombeaux' (1852), which grieves over the fact that Christianity
opposes 'the gods whom art always reveres': artistically, it is
a sad day when 'Olympus yields to Calvary,/Jupiter to the
Nazarean', and self-denial comes to rank more highly than
sensuous exuberance. D'Albert, the hero of Gautier's novel
(and Swinburne's bible) *Mademoiselle de Maupin* (1835),

expresses many of those aesthetico-pagan sentiments later epitomized in Ezra Pound's 'Hugh Selwyn Mauberley' (1920), where the replacement of a phallic and ambrosial paganism by the macerations of Christian asceticism is held responsible for a narrowing of awareness and a subsequent depression of artistic possibilities.

Friedrich Schiller was among the first to testify to this nostalgia for a lost mythology which the arts must recover if they are to survive. His poem written in the 1790s on 'The Gods of Greece' expresses such sympathy for the spirit of paganism that Elizabeth Barrett Browning was 'excited' (her own word) to answer it with an impassioned but mediocre poem called 'The Dead Pan' (1844). Schiller anticipates Gautier in equating art with beauty and beauty with paganism. He mourns the iridescence which has vanished from a world deprived of its gods (*entgötterte Natur*), and offers asylum in literature to those gods the world now deems redundant. Similar tones of regret run through a passage in the second play (*Die Piccolomini*) of Schiller's trilogy, *Wallenstein* (1799), a passage brought to the attention of English readers in the version by Coleridge (1800), which Scott thought so exquisite that he incorporated it into the third chapter of *Guy Mannering* (1815) when evoking the ruins of Ellgowan castle by moonlight. The pagan gods, writes Schiller,

> live no longer in the faith of reason!
> But still the heart doth need a language, still
> Doth the old instinct bring back the old names. (II. iv)

In more down-to-earth language, this is tantamount to saying that the gods survive because their names survive, and so a new mythological theme is created: where are the gods now, and what have they been doing all this time? Heinrich Heine writes engagingly on this problem in 'The Gods in Exile' (1853). Alternating irony with nostalgia (for he was no stranger to the conflicting sentiments engendered by exile),

Heine pretends to scour medieval legends for news of what happened to the pagan gods after Christianity enforced their diaspora. He finds that some were fortunate, like Pluto, who could lie low in his underworld; Neptune, too, was generally out of earshot of church-bells and organs. Others, however, declined lamentably. Apollo was obliged to work as a shepherd in Austria, whereas Jupiter lived alone with his tattered eagle somewhere in the arctic circle, trading rabbit-skins with Laplanders. The wily ones fared rather better. Bacchus and a couple of Sileni had no difficulty in becoming Franciscan monks; but the most successful exile by far (Heine makes no comment on the transit of Venus) was the psychopomp Mercury, who established himself in the Dutch conveyance business and there, taking a hint from Procopius (*History of the Wars*, VIII. xx. 48), developed a highly lucrative scheme for shipping the souls of the dead to the fortunate isles of Great Britain. Walter Pater was intrigued, and described a thirteenth-century resurgence of Dionysus in 'Denys L'Auxerrois' (1886). In 'Apollo in Picardy' (1893) the god reappears on a monastic farm in medieval Picardy, where he is known by the same name as the angel of the bottomless pit, Apollyon (Revelation, 9:11). Here Pater draws on the tradition established by St Justin Martyr (in his *First Apology*, liv) that all the pagan gods were demons who fell with Lucifer, which makes the Greeks contemptible in having nothing more than 'devils to adore for deities' (*Paradise Lost*, i. 373).

But there was no need to suppose that the old gods had not been seen since the Middle Ages. It was simply a question of knowing how and where to look for them. Visit the Mediterranean with Ezra Pound, for instance, and you may still see 'gods float in the azure air' (Canto 3). Indeed, as recently as 1958 Orpheus was discovered alive and well and working as a tram-driver in Rio de Janeiro, where he was filmed by Marcel Camus (*Black Orpheus*). And sightings of Pan have been reported in such profusion that Somerset Maugham was

driven to disparage them in *Cakes and Ale* (London, 1930):
'Poets saw him lurking in the twilight on London commons,
and literary ladies in Surrey and New England, nymphs of an
industrial age, mysteriously surrendered their virginity to his
rough embrace. Spiritually, they were never the same again'
(ch. 11). Nor could they be, for in such an ethos it was time to
reconsider Plutarch's account of the death of Pan (*Moralia*,
419). Leigh Hunt could look forward to the day when 'a
voice will be heard along the water saying "The great god Pan
is alive again"' (letter to Hogg, 22 January 1818); but it was
James Thomson who first parodied Plutarch's phrase exactly
in his polemical essay, 'Great Christ is Dead!' (1875), shortly
before Nietzsche's Madman was to run through the pages of
Die Froeliche Wissenschaft (1882) proclaiming that 'God is
dead!' (paragraph 125).

Revivalists soon discover that nostalgia is not enough, and
worry about the problems of archaism. Elizabeth Barrett told
Robert Browning that the new age demanded 'new *forms*, as
well as thoughts', and that it was pointless to 'go back to the
antique moulds, classical moulds, as they are so improperly
called' (20 March 1845). Tennyson agreed. 'It is no use giving
a mere *réchauffé* of old legends', he remarked when discussing
'Demeter and Persephone' (1889) with his son. Somehow, a
modern writer must learn to rehabilitate Demeter without, as
it were, purveying the concomitant corn. One solution is to
dismantle the forms of pagan mythology in the hope of re-
covering the state of mind which first created them. This is
what William Carlos Williams envisages in *A Voyage to
Pagany* (New York, 1928), where Pagany is a collective name
for the Europe which produced pagan mythologies. Instead of
boring everybody with yet another account of Orpheus, you
present an orphic situation – a mermaid singing, for instance,

> Uttering such dulcet and harmonious breath,
> That the rude sea grew civil at her song . . . .
> (*A Midsummer-Night's Dream*, II. i. 150f.)

And in a New World where mermaids have never been sighted, Wallace Stevens can still recapture an orphic moment in Florida, when a singing girl imposes an idea of order at Key West. 'Start with the sun', advises Bernice Slote, echoing D. H. Lawrence: 'perhaps then we may be absolved from the poetry of mirrors' (*Start With the Sun* [Lincoln, 1960], p. 238).

New mythologies

Disturbed at the increasing fragmentariness of modern poetry, Friedrich Schlegel called in his 'Talk on Mythology' (1800) for the creation of a new mythology which might unify modern literature in the way that classical mythology had formerly unified the literature of the Ancients. Exactly where it was to come from was uncertain. On the one hand he expected it to be fashioned from the profoundest depths of the spirit (*aus der tiefsten Tiefe des Geistes*), and on the other hand he envisaged revitalization from the exotic and barely known mythologies of India: 'in the Orient we must look for the most sublime form of the Romantic' (1800, p. 87). Like all important prophecies, Schlegel's was comprehensive enough to come true, no matter what happened; so it was hardly fair of him to be right on both counts. For the deepest depths of the human spirit were soon to be plumbed by the depth-psychology (*Tiefenpsychologie*) of Freud, who concluded that 'the theory of the instincts is . . . our mythology' (*CPW*, xxii, p. 95); and Willson's book on the Indian elements in German Romanticism describes the extraordinary impact on German letters of Georg Forster's German version (1791) of Sir William Jones's English translation (1789) of Calidasa's *Sacontala*.

Was it necessary to go quite so far afield? Perhaps not. Northern Europeans bored with the mythologies of southern Europe could always turn to the indigenous mythologies of northern Europe, especially after Paul Henri Mallet had made available the Nordic mythology of the *Eddas* in the second volume of his *Introduction à l'Histoire du Danemarc* (Copenhagen, 1756), which Thomas Percy translated as *Northern Antiquities* (London, 1770). Potentially invaluable to anybody interested in creating a national literature free from the imaginative tyranny of Greece, Nordic mythology was unfortunately flawed in the eyes of neoclassicists by what Edward Williams called its 'superlatively barbarous and bloody theology' (*Poems, Lyric and Personal* [London, 1794], preface). Some eighty years later, William Morris was still feeling obliged to tone down *The Story of Sigurd the Volsung* (1876) for an age which found even Greek mythology so grossly improper that it tolerated such bowdlerized handbooks as Charles Kingsley's *The Heroes* (Cambridge, 1855) – admittedly for children – and Thomas Bulfinch's *The Age of Fable* (Boston, 1855). How much easier it was in the late eighteenth century to vibrate sympathetically to something as elegantly bogus as the Ossianic poetry allegedly translated from the Gaelic of the 'Homer of the North', but in fact cleverly counterfeited by James Macpherson in a series of works beginning with *Fragments of Ancient Poetry Collected in the Highlands of Scotland* (Edinburgh, 1760). Snyder's book on the Celtic Revival (1923) shows that very few of those who drifted from dryads to Druids knew the difference between Celtic and Norse mythologies, with the result that fictional Druids risked being consigned at death to Valhalla. In any case, the new mythology contributed little to poetry except new names, for Plinlimmon was likely to be given the same 'cloud-topped head' which formerly had adorned Olympus or Parnassus. Even Thomas Gray, who kept the Celtic theme of 'The Bard' (1754–7) scrupulously apart from the Norse of 'The Descent of Odin' (1761), levelled their differences by writing about them in the same neoclassical manner he used for all his poems. His own ambition in such pieces is betrayed in an absurd compliment crediting William Mason with the

invention of 'a new mythology peculiar to the Druid super-
stition, and not borrowed of the Greeks' (letter 239, June
1757). In addition to the technical difficulties of finding new
ways of writing about the newly discovered mythologies, there
was also the problem of suspending disbelief in them. William
Collins' remarkable 'Ode on the Popular Superstitions of the
Highlands of Scotland' (written in 1749) suggests it is all very
well for somebody like John Home to occupy himself with
'false themes', because his fellow-countrymen still believe in
them; but a sophisticated Englishman has really no justification for perpetuating superstitious nonsense.

Meanwhile, theoretical foundations were being laid for the
establishment of Druidic mythology as the aboriginal and
therefore 'native' mythology of the British Isles, as well as
the ultimate source even of Greek mythology – thus strengthen-
ing Milton's opinion that 'the school of Pythagoras and the
Persian wisdom took beginning from the old philosophy of
this island' (*Areopagitica*, 1644). The theme of William
Stukeley's book on *Stonehenge* (London, 1740) is that Druids
came to Britain 'during the life of the patriarch Abraham, or
very soon after' (p. 2), bringing with them certain 'Diluvian
truths and patriarchal lore' whose decay Wordsworth laments
in the third of his *Ecclesiastical Sonnets* (1822). Hungerford
(1941) reconstructs the making of the neodruidic heresy that
medieval Welsh and Irish bards were descended from a bardic
class of patriarchal Druids. If we still pay attention to any
of this nonsense, it is largely because William Blake was convinced by it. Blake read the work of Celtomanes like Stukeley
in the light of Jacob Bryant, whose *New System . . . of Ancient
Mythology* (London, 1774–6) backs up the old patristic view
that the Greeks did not invent their own myths, and argues a
Babylonian origin for Greek mythology. And by the time
Edward Davies had established that Druids were in Britain
even before the Flood, the most ancient history could con-
fidently be said to have taken place in Britain, which became

ipso facto the seat of all ancient wisdom. Hence Blake could fulminate in *Milton* (1804–8) against 'the stolen and perverted writings of Homer and Ovid, of Plato and Cicero', and evoke those distant days when the holy lamb of God was to be seen on England's pleasant pastures.

Blake is the most impressive writer to draw on the researches of the so-called 'speculative mythologists' whose comparative studies had the effect of rebarbarizing the Greek pantheon. Other writers owe little more than the occasional detail to contemporary theorists, as Keats does in *Hyperion* when making his Titaness Asia the daughter of Caf; or when Shelley conflates the Greek Adonis with Hebrew *adonai* ('lords') in 'Adonais'. What is displayed here is a characteristic-ally English caution in quietly syncretizing the new with the old. Just as in earlier centuries medieval writers had mingled classical nymphs with Celtic fairies without feeling obliged to make a proclamation about it, so too the young Byron could confess in *The Island* (ii. 12) to having

> Mixed Celtic memories with the Phrygian mount,
> And Highland linns with Castalie's clear fount.

Despite the allurements of exotic pantheons, English writers on the whole remained faithful to classical mythology, how-ever threadbare it was becoming.

If none of the available mythologies proves satisfactory, you can always invent your own, taking heart from what Los says in Blake's *Jerusalem* (1804–20): 'I must create a system or be enslaved by another man's' (i. 10). The end-product may be an eclectic synopticon like W. B. Yeats's *A Vision* (London, 1937) or Robert Graves's *The White Goddess* (London, 1961), or less flamboyantly a creation-myth like *The Prelude* (1805), which is Wordsworth's personal cosmogony. Clean breaks with allegedly extinct mythologies are hard to achieve, to judge from evidence amassed in source-studies devoted to Blake and Yeats, and the mythopoeic impulse in imaginations as powerful as those of James Joyce or Thomas Mann may be impeded by a reluctance to let go of traditional mythologies (Herd, 1969, p. 74f.). Mythopoesis is the growth-point of a mythology, but hazardous to those who cultivate it. In the first place, the strain of manufacturing a Schlegelian mythology out of the deepest depths of the spirit is enormous, for you end up with Gottfried Benn papering the walls with your own skin, while psychoanalytic critics stand around discussing your obsessive imagery (Mauron) and mulling over Freud's remark that mythopoeic impulses manifest themselves nowadays in the form of neuroses (*CPW*, xii, p. 82). An equally serious drawback in trying to go it alone is evident to any reader of Blake's *The Four Zoas* or Ezra Pound's *Cantos*, and it is this: a mythology you invent does not have the resonances of one you inherit, and must always remain private except to the happy few who take the trouble to work it out. This is why people who believe that myths are 'collective representations' in Durkheim's sense think it impossible for any one person to be credited with the invention of a myth. 'What such modern writers as Melville or Kafka create is not myth', according to Hyman, 'but an individual fantasy expressing a symbolic action, equivalent to and related to the myth's expression of a public rite. No one, not even Melville . . . can invent myths' (1966, p. 57). The problem is first raised in Book 3 of Vico's *Scienza Nuova* (1725–44), where 'Homer' is treated as the work of a whole people instead of a single poet; and ballads were later to be looked upon as some sort of communal poetizing on the part of the folk (*das Volk dichtet*). Ultimately, such speculations lead to the collectivist mysticism of Jane Harrison's remark that 'myth is a fragment of the soul-life, the dream-thinking of the people, as the dream is the myth of the individual' (*Epilegomena to the Study of Greek Religion* [Cambridge, 1921], p. 32). But surely a myth is initially as much the work of an individual as a ballad is or an epic poem: somebody has to supply the raw material which others may then add to and alter. Braswell finds mythological innovation already present in Homer's treatment of Thetis in the *Iliad*; and we can all think of mythical figures which are known to be the invention of particular authors, such as Jekyll and Hyde (R. L. Stevenson), Frankenstein (Mary Shelley), Dracula (Bram Stoker) and Rip Van Winkle (Washington Irving). Interestingly enough, they are not usually recalled in their bookish context, but thought of as wholly traditional figures in the public domain of horror-movies and comic strips; before very long Frankenstein is no longer remembered as the name of Mary Shelley's 'modern Prometheus' but popularly confused with the monster he created. Here, possibly, we have a paradigm of the processes by which myths are made.

4

Myths and critics

Thematology is that branch of literary studies which attracts people who aspire to something more ambitious than the mythographer's humble task of collecting and collating myths in all their variant forms. The thematological study of myths is a discipline in the hands of literary comparatists, and consitutes a reputable subdivision of *Stoffgeschichte*. Thematologists usually select the stories associated with one of the more celebrated figures from classical mythology, and then study what happens to them when they are retold by a wide variety of European writers from antiquity to the present day: one thinks of Trousson's exemplary study of Prometheus (1964), or Galinsky's of Heracles (1972), or Stanford's of Ulysses (1954). Alternatively, they may take a mythological theme, as Levin does in his beautifully written study of the Golden Age in the Renaissance (1970), and submit that to the same treatment. What distinguishes such enquiries from nineteenth-century examples of the comparative method, like E. S. Hartland's study of *The Legend of Perseus* (London, 1894–6), is their endeavour to treat the stories told about Greek heroes as emic totalities, and to resist fragmenting them into etic components, each of which may be shown to belong to a large family of non-European analogues, including such non-literary sources as folklore. Provided one avoids the mistake of assuming that any version which deviates from the earliest recorded form of a myth is thereby a perversion of the 'original', literary study has much to gain from investigating what Munz calls the 'typological seriality' (1973, p. 28) of emically constituted myths. Apart from inviting literary historians to speculate as to why certain myths disappear and reappear when they do, thematologists enable us to see exactly what aspects of a myth have been emphasized in the writings of any particular author, and may confirm or provoke some insight into his work, as happens when Merivale places selected fiction by D. H. Lawrence in the context of the Pan myth (1969). One drawback of thematological studies is that an obligation to be comprehensive often means that a disproportionate amount of space must be allotted to minor writers and their minimal works. Another drawback, equally unavoidable, is that all such studies teach more or less the same lesson: all myths go through much the same stages in mirroring the different preoccupations of different ages, with the result that a diachronic analysis of any one of the enduring myths provides a model for all the rest.

Myth-criticism

The general tendency of thematological studies is to emphasize the craftsmanship of writing by implying that authors consciously select the myths they explore. Thematologists look upon mythology as a patrimony providing workable subject-matter, their assumption being that myths are there to be used by anybody who wants to use them. They do not imagine, as many myth-critics seem to do, that writers are somehow possessed by the myths they recount (or invent) by virtue of some unique ability to think 'mythically' in an age which has aspired since Socratic times to think rationally. The basic difference between these two approaches to the presence of mythology in literature is brought out very clearly by Philip Rahv in dissenting from myth-critical approaches to the novels of Thomas Mann: '*Joseph and His Brothers* is not so much a mythic novel as a novel on mythic themes' (1953, p. 645).

What people mean by 'mythic consciousness' is traceable usually to the second volume of Ernst Cassirer's *Philosophy of Symbolic Forms* (1925), a book which is ostensibly a work of philosophy but (as references to Schelling make clear) is in fact a late and sophisticated contribution to Romantic speculations about the expressive powers and picturesque vividness of language in a so-called primitive state. Cassirer treats myth as a primordial 'symbolic form', that is, as one of those things (like language itself) which we interpose between ourselves and the outside world in order to apprehend it: to him, myth is a non-discursive, densely imagistic 'language', not unlike the language of Freudian dreams, at once more archaic and vibrant than that cerebral and discursive language in which Cassirer's own book is written. If myth is the primal language of experience, modern writers who explore the recesses of mythic consciousness and deposit their findings in works of fiction should be valued for keeping us vitally in touch with the very springs of our humanity; or so the story goes. But how do Cassirer and his admirers know all this? Nobody has ever met an archaic man, so his mental habits must remain entirely conjectural, and anthropologists insist that we ought not to regard present-day primitive man as a living remnant of archaic man (Herskovits, 1958, p. 82f.). Where then is the evidence for 'mythical thought' if not in Lucien Lévy-Bruhl's theory of 'primitive mentality'? And as we have no way of demonstrating that the mythopoeic ability of a modern writer is an archaic residue (or even a primitive one, for that matter), there is not much point in saying it is unless one happens to thrill at the very suggestion that primitive vestiges are present in modern man. One can no more treat *The Philosophy of Symbolic Forms* as an objective study of primitive mentality than one can regard William Golding's novel *The Inheritors* (London, 1955) as a dramatized documentary study of life in a Neanderthal tribe, whose people are animistic in outlook, think imagistically, talk picturesquely, and are innately good into the bargain. Both works are highly imaginative projections, in very different forms, of the same basically Romantic conviction that myth is endemic to primitive mentality.

It is characteristic of myth-criticism to turn attention away from the local specificities of a particular book towards some myth which is held to be older and grander and therefore better than the book one is actually talking about. What might have been a mere novel ('only a novel') suddenly becomes Literature as its author is shown to transcend the quotidian and make contact with the eternal by way of some archetypal image or situation already familiar in mythology. It is seen to be Scott Fitzgerald's distinction not to have evoked the frenetic glamour of the Jazz Age in *The Great Gatsby* (New York, 1925) but to have refurbished the American Adam. Yet however little we know about Jay Gatsby, we know considerably more about him than we do about Adam. This raises the question as to what value there can be in a method of literary analysis which, in reaching towards some indistinct archetype, turns aside from those ectypal particularities which make a novel uniquely what it is. 'One central principle of myth-criticism', according to Vickery, 'is that the individual and universal forms of an image are identical' (1966, p. 96). How could this ever be determined, I wonder, seeing that we have no access to the universal except by way of the particular? What seems to be more truly the aim of myth-criticism is to establish a system of reductive monism for the reintegration of the Many into the One. The title of Joseph Campbell's book, *The Hero With a Thousand Faces* (1949), is revealing in this respect: not a thousand different heroes, but just one, who appears in a thousand different guises, as Isis Myrionyma is known by a multiplicity of names. And it is equally significant that a fascination with archetypal images has led some to intensify their reductive approach by seeking to locate the Archetype behind the archetypes, what Campbell calls the 'monomyth' (1949, p. 10), a term he takes from *Finnegans*

Wake. If the Joycean context fails to clarify the meaning of 'monomyth', Campbell's book reveals that the fundamental mythic pattern is the *rite de passage* first described by Arnold van Gennep in 1909: 'the standard path of the mythological adventure of the hero is a magnification of the formula represented in the rites of passage: *separation-initiation-return*; which may be named the nuclear unit of the monomyth', and is further glossed as 'a separation from the world, a penetration to some source of power, and a life-enhancing return' (1949, pp. 30, 35). Impressive enough as a monomyth, it has not gone unrivalled: Raglan (1936) prefers a monomyth derived from an *ur*-ritual celebrating the Dying God, as described in the fourth volume of Frazer's *Golden Bough;* to Róheim, 'the nucleus of myth is the death and apotheosis of the Primal Father' (*American Imago*, ii [1941], p. 278), whereas Eliade seems to favour the myth of Creation.

By far the most popular monomyth among literary critics has been the quest-myth, especially since 1951, when Northrop Frye first identified it as the central myth of literature and the source of all literary genres. Tactically, the choice of quest-myth as monomyth was excellent, for a nascent myth-criticism had to make its way when New Criticism was dominant, and a couple of New Criticism's most hallowed texts are demonstrably quest-myths of 1922 vintage: Joyce's *Ulysses* and Eliot's *The Waste Land*, the latter openly inviting comparison (if not altogether illuminating comparison) with Jessie L. Weston's study of the Grail Quest in *From Ritual to Romance* (Cambridge, 1920). If readers were to be weaned away from a New Critical preoccupation with formal properties (like irony, tension and paradox) to rediscover the content of literature by reference to archetypal imagery, then *Ulysses* and *The Waste Land* were as good a place to start as any: for had not Eliot himself praised Joyce in 1923 for having invented a 'mythical method' or 'continuous parallel between contemporaneity and antiquity' which enables a modern writer to give 'a shape and a significance to the immense panorama of futility and anarchy which is contemporary history' (1965, p. 681)? Since then, the epigoni of myth-criticism have stultified us with revelations of hitherto unsuspected quest-myths: 'anybody who goes looking for anything becomes a participant in a "quest-myth",' Hough complains (1966, p. 143); so it would be merciful of them to declare a moratorium on quests, and give one of the other monomyths a run for a while.

Although it is salutary to be reminded every now and then that literature has content as well as form, it is not certain that literature is enhanced by the kind of content which attracts myth-critics. A method which homogenizes books in order to apprehend the supernal one-ness of things can easily become monotonous in practice, effacing the element of surprise from literature and instituting in its place a *déjà-vu*. Just as Curtius' *topoi* are literally commonplaces and therefore commonplace, so too the cant use of 'archetype' is a euphemism for cliché. Wimsatt justly objects that 'to describe Hamlet's stage-tradition jump into Ophelia's grave as if it were an instance of the classic descent into the underworld is a cliché application of the archetype, ingenious perhaps, but still a cliché, a mythopoeist's cliché' (1966, p. 95). Besides, archetypal images are not intrinsically valuable, and may pop up in a toothpaste advertisement as readily as in an epic poem. This is why one appreciates Fiedler's point that the signature on an archetype is much more important than the archetype itself. And awareness of the historical context in which archetypal images occur is equally necessary if one is to avoid the kind of errors Moorman castigates (1956) in interpretations of *Sir Gawain and the Green Knight* by Jungians and ritualists. All too easily, myth-criticism displays the weaknesses of old-fashioned source-studies, with the added disadvantage of being unable to point to anything as tangible as a literary text. One need only consider the usual treatment accorded William Faulkner's *The Bear*, a story which has very much the look of stories that

are looked at: 'beneath its other layers of meaning', writes
Lydenberg, 'the story is essentially a nature myth' (1952–3,
p. 63). But that word 'essentially' refers to something which
is quite spectral in comparison with what goes on in our minds
as we read Faulkner's story. Perhaps such errors arise from
the centralizing of elements which are merely peripheral, with
the result that a suggestion comes to be read as an affirmation,
a nuance crystallizes into a leitmotif, part of the background
moves centre-stage, and quite athwart goes all decorum.

Obviously, it is not easy to invent a critical language capable
of straddling the ectypal and the archetypal, which is why
myth-critics have unwittingly made some delightful contribu-
tions to the art of sinking. The dreary earnestness of so much
myth-critical writing may be relieved unexpectedly, as it is
when Blotner dutifully explains that 'whereas Rhea has six
children, three boys and three girls, Mrs Ramsay has eight,
four boys and four girls' (1956, p. 551). Discounting such
lapses, however, there is little doubt that many people find the
language of myth-criticism attractive, for it resounds with
awe-inspiring words like 'primeval', 'mana', 'preternatural',
'matrix', 'archetypal', 'primordial' – words which promise to
take us far away from the Romantic hearts and New Critical
heads of mere time-bound readers and put us directly in touch
with the eternal and infinite and Wholly Other. The closest
precedent to a criticism operating on such a grandiose scale is
in the aesthetics of the sublime, centred as it is in the recognition of terrified wonder in the presence of vague immensities.
Just how swiftly myth-criticism degenerates into a rhetorical
trick for soliciting tacit approval among the converted is
demonstrated in an essay on *Moby Dick* reprinted in Vickery's
anthology (1966, pp. 193–9), which talks glibly about Ahab's
'ceremonial rituals' and 'talismanic lance', and points to
'mythopoeic scenes' in which Ahab reacts 'preternaturally' or
briefs his crew 'shamanistically'. If this tells us nothing at all
about Melville the writer, it undoubtedly reassures readers in

search of archetypal sensations that *Moby Dick* is their kind of book.

The point made implicitly in Douglas Bush's amusing parody of myth-criticism (1956) is that the jargon applies only to selected books, and certainly not to *Pride and Prejudice*. While an archetypal analysis of Shelley's *Prometheus Unbound* is feasible enough, *The Canterbury Tales* are not susceptible to such treatment, despite the fact that they record a pilgrimage and so qualify as a quest. As Righter observes, it can hardly be coincidental that myth-criticism is largely an American phenomenon, encouraged by the overtly symbolic or allegorical mode of nineteenth-century American literature (1972–3, p. 324). In more recent times, much American fiction looks as if it was designed for the kind of inspection it now receives: one thinks of Ernest Hemingway's *The Old Man and the Sea* (New York, 1952), a book practically tailor-made for undergraduate analysis – not too long, and chock-a-block with symbols, each one as carefully planted as a Piltdown skull. With so many willing explicators in attendance, how many writers can claim with Vladimir Nabokov to have produced 'mythproof' fictions, around which 'Freudians flutter . . . avidly, approach with itching oviducts, stop, sniff, and recoil' (*The Eye* [London, 1966], p. 9)? As always, tone is the biggest obstacle to a fully automated myth-criticism. When Bernard Malamud mixed Grail materials with baseball in his novel *The Natural* (New York, 1952), there was some uncertainty as to whether he was being pretentious (Dalziel) or ironic; and when John Updike published *The Centaur* (New York, 1963) he provided a 'Mythological Index' to the novel which is at once helpful and a spoof of essays offering that kind of help. In retrospect, the tone of *Ulysses* is comparatively straightforward, and it is hard to imagine how people ever came to misunderstand (in ways Joseph von Abele describes) the ironies of its mythological allusions. Nowadays, when the deep readers of the world descend on any new work by a reputable novelist, writers cultivate an elusive tone in order to avoid being type-cast. Parts of *Henderson the Rain King* (New York, 1958) may be read as an orthodox quest-novel, complete with Frazerian trimmings; other parts read like a parody of quest-novels; and while we argue about which tone is the dominant one, Bellow lives to write another day.

Now if several books can be discussed in terms of the one myth, it follows that all books might well be classified by the myths to which they allude, in which case one might treat the wide spectrum of tales told in universal mythologies as providing a new system of literary classification to replace such traditional genres as the epic, drama, lyric and so on. The most ambitious attempt to construct a new taxonomy for literature on mythic principles is Northrop Frye's *Anatomy of Criticism* (1957), which treats 'the symbolism of the Bible, and to a lesser extent classical mythology, as a grammar of literary archetypes' (p. 135): literature is 'displaced' mythology, best understood if replaced in its correct mythical context. The purpose of undertaking such a scheme is to stimulate fresh insights into individual books by juxtaposing them with others belonging to the same category, but the enterprise is beset by a couple of practical difficulties. In the first place, we can never be sure that we have classified a work correctly: is Keats's 'La Belle Dame Sans Merci' a Tannhäuser or Melusina myth? And even if we classify it correctly, we may find that books bearing the same shelf-mark in the new system are so different from one another ectypally that their selection might just as well have been random. What does Fielding's *Tom Jones* have in common with Voltaire's *Candide*, Alain-Fournier's *Le Grand Meaulnes*, Galsworthy's *The Apple Tree* and Eichendorff's *Aus dem Leben eines Taugenichts?* The answer, according to Manfred Sandmann (1966), is that all are mutations of the Percival archetype. Frye's book, however, is altogether more macroscopic than this in outlook, conflating the traditional genres with seasonal symbolism and providing accommodation for any book ever written. Although it has a Thomist look about it, Frye's *summa* is pragmatic in intention: 'the system was there for the insights it contained', he reminded members of the English Institute who met to discuss his work; 'the insights were not there for the sake of the system' (Krieger, 1966, p. 28). Yet anybody who uses the index to *Anatomy of Criticism* in the hope of acquiring insights into particular books is in for disappointments: the two entries on Trollope, for instance, tell us only that Trollope wrote novels which were read as romances during the Second World War (pp. 305, 307). Literary works and their authors merit a mention in Frye's book only by qualifying as examples of something or other in his system: it is the system which is the insight, the vision of literature in its entirety as a vast spatial design, beautiful in its coherence, autonomous, and ultimately autotelic. *Anatomy of Criticism* is a work of synoptic finality, and of comparable status in the realm of criticism to those showpieces of Alexandrian modernism, *The Waste Land* and *Ulysses*, although written more along the lines of Yeats' *A Vision*. Far from fulfilling the Linnaean ambition of providing a *taxonomia universalis* for literature, *Anatomy of Criticism* is itself a triumph of the mythopoeic imagination, a beautifully modulated address to an Academy of Fine Ideas, but not much use to the practising critic, who will find in John J. White's excellent book on *Mythology and the Modern Novel* (1972) far more helpful advice on how to talk about myths as they appear in works of fiction.

Postscript

Folklorists, who once collaborated happily enough with literary students by investigating the hinterland of popular customs and beliefs at which authors traditionally glance, are now openly contemptuous of the way the word 'myth' is bandied about by irresponsible literati. Stith Thompson (1958, p. 104) complains of 'perversions of the word "myth"' by certain unnamed literary critics, perhaps the same ones Fontenrose has difficulty in understanding because their conception of myth is 'so vague as to be useless' (1971, p. 56). As newly emergent social scientists, folklorists are understandably prone to definitional anxieties, and are quite right in thinking that many literary critics are hopelessly muddled about myth. But this is really beside the point. The fact is that literary terms cast their shadows diachronically and are therefore capable of meaning anything they have been thought to mean in the past, or are thought to mean right now. Nothing would be gained by formulating a brand-new synchronic definition of myth and insisting that everybody accept it. What we really need is an understanding of those conflicting interests which have contributed to the present muddle. Was it the very ambiguities of "myth" which first attracted those engaged in the increasingly desperate endeavour of finding new ways of defending imaginative literature against enemies ancient and modern? Such is Kermode's diagnosis: 'in the dominion of myth', he writes, 'we can short-circuit the intellect and liberate the imagination which the scientism of the modern world suppresses; and this is the central modern position' (1962, p. 37). Or is the aesthetic issue merely a front for more ambitious and even sinister operations? Philip Rahv, for instance, sees in myth-criticism a sort of *ersatz* religion dreamed up by people who cannot tolerate the chaos of history (the 'powerhouse' of change) and so take refuge in the stability of myth; Roland Barthes believes that 'the very end of myths is to immobilize the world' (1972, p. 155). Looked at in this light, to be preoccupied with myth reveals a yearning for order in the midst of upheavals and fragmentariness. 'What the myth-critics appear to seek', says Paul West, 'is a kind of philosopher's stone which turns all conflict into golden myth', a myth which 'enables us to live out our lives intelligently in the presence of suggested pattern' (1961, p. 365f.). And if the pattern is the status quo, as it must be, myth-criticism stands revealed as the organ of bourgeois reactionaries. Kogan assails the Fascist premises of a literary method which bases itself unashamedly on a racist theory of archetypes and delays the overthrow of American imperialism by perpetuating belief in its eternal recurrence. All is not lost, however, because 'the practice of archetypal criticism is limited exclusively to the corridors of intellectually bankrupt U.S. imperialist universities, and the number of practitioners of archetypal criticism is very small even among academic hacks' (1970, p. 29). Reluctant to identify myself as the *hypocrite lecteur* Kogan castigates, I can only point lamely to the foregoing pages as evidence that anybody who decides to deepen his understanding of literature by taking an eclectic interest in myth is in no real danger of emerging from his studies as a hot-gospeller, crypto-fascist, or even a folklorist, unless he was that way inclined to begin with. For as long as myth remains the patrimony of the arts, we shall do well to know something about it.

Bibliography

Allen, Don Cameron (1970) *Mysteriously Meant* The rediscovery of pagan symbolism and allegorical interpretation in the Renaissance. Baltimore & London.

Allen, James Lovic (1973–4) 'The Road to Byzantium: Archetypal Criticism and Yeats', *Journal of Aesthetics and Art Criticism*, xxxii, pp. 53–64.

Ashmole, Elias (comp.) (1967) *Theatrum Chemicum Britannicum* Containing several poetical pieces of our famous English philosophers, who have written the Hermetic mysteries in their own ancient language (London, 1652); facsimile repr. intro. Allen G. Debus. New York & London.

Barthes, Roland (1972) *Mythologies* Selected & trans. Annette Lavers. London.

Belli, Angela (1969) *Ancient Greek Myths and Modern Drama* A study in continuity. New York & London.

Bidney, David (1953) *Theoretical Anthropology* New York. Ch. 10: The concept of myth.

Blotner, Joseph L. (1956) 'Mythic Patterns in *To the Lighthouse*', *PMLA*, lxxi, pp. 547–62.

Boccaccio, Giovanni (1930) *Boccaccio on Poetry* Being the Preface and the Fourteenth and Fifteenth Books of Boccaccio's *Genealogia Deorum Gentilium* in an English version, with introductory essay and commentary by Charles G. Osgood. Princeton.

Bodkin, Maud (1934) *Archetypal Patterns in Poetry* Psychological studies of imagination. London.

Boewe, Charles (1961) 'Myth and Literary Studies', *University of Kansas City Review*, xxvii, pp. 191–6.

Bolle, Kees W. (1970) 'In Defense of Euhemerus' in *Myth and Law Among the Indo-Europeans* Studies in Indo-European comparative mythology. Ed. Jaan Puhvel. Berkeley. pp. 19–38.

Boon, James A. (1972) *From Symbolism to Structuralism* Lévi-Strauss in a literary tradition. Oxford.

Braswell, B. K. (1971) 'Mythological Innovation in the *Iliad*', *Classical Quarterly*, xxxi, pp. 16–26.

Brinkley, Roberta Florence (1932) *Arthurian Legend in the Seventeenth Century*. Baltimore.

Brown, Daniel Russell (1969–70) 'A Look at Archetypal Criticism', *Journal of Aesthetics and Art Criticism*, xxviii, pp. 465–72.

Brown, Truesdell S. (1946) 'Euhemerus and the Historians', *Harvard Theological Review*, xxxix, pp. 259–74.

Budick, S. (1970) 'The Demythological Mode in Augustan Verse', *ELH*, xxxvii, pp. 389–414.

Bultmann, Rudolf (1961) *Kerygma and Myth* A theological debate. Ed. Hans Werner Bartsch. Trans. Reginald H. Fuller. New York.

Bush, Douglas (1932) *Mythology and the Renaissance Tradition in English Poetry* Minneapolis.

Bush, Douglas (1937) *Mythology and the Romantic Tradition in English Poetry* Cambridge, Mass.

Bush, Douglas (1956) 'Mrs Bennet and the Dark Gods: the Truth about Jane Austen', *Sewanee Review*, lxiv, pp. 591–6.

Bush, Douglas (1968) *Pagan Myth and Christian Tradition in English Poetry* Philadelphia.

Joseph, Campbell (1949) *The Hero With a Thousand Faces* New York.

Capell, A. (1938–9) 'The Word "Mana": a Linguistic Study', *Oceania*, ix, pp. 89–96.

Cassirer, Ernst (1946) *Language and Myth* Trans. Susanne K. Langer. New York & London.

Cassirer, Ernst (1955) *The Philosophy of Symbolic Forms* Vol. 2: *Mythical Thought* Trans. Ralph Manheim. New Haven.

Chapman, George (1957) *Chapman's Homer* The *Iliad*, the *Odyssey* and the Lesser Homerica. Ed., intro, and notes by Allardyce Nicoll. London. 2 vols.

Chase, Richard (1948) 'Myth as Literature' in *English Institute Essays, 1947* Ed. D. A. Robertson. New York. pp. 3–22.

Chase, Richard (1949) *Quest for Myth* Baton Rouge.

Chase, Richard (1957) *The American Novel and its Tradition* London. Appendix 2: Romance, the folk imagination and myth criticism.

Cohen, Percy S. (1969) 'Theories of Myth', *Man*, n.s., iv, pp. 337–53.

Cooke, J. D. (1927) 'Euhemerism: A Mediaeval Interpretation of Classical Paganism', *Speculum*, ii, pp. 396–410.

Cunningham, Adrian (ed.) (1974). *The Theory of Myth* Six Studies. London.

Curry, Walter C. (1923) 'Astrologising the Gods', *Anglia*, xlvii, pp. 213–43.

Daiches, David (1968) *More Literary Essays* London. pp. 1–18: Myth, metaphor, and poetry.

Dalziel, Margaret (ed.) (1967) *Myth and the Modern Imagination* Dunedin, N.Z.

Dickinson, Hugh (1969) *Myth on the Modern Stage* Urbana.

Donno, Elizabeth Story (ed. & intro.) (1963) *Elizabethan Minor Epics* London.

Douglas, W. W. (1952–3) 'The Meanings of "Myth" in Modern Criticism', *Modern Philology*, 1, pp. 232–42.

Eisenstein, Samuel A. (1968) 'Literature and Myth', *College English*, xxix, pp. 369–73.

Eliade, Mircea (1954) *The Myth of the Eternal Return* Trans. W. R. Trask. New York.

Eliot, T. S. (1923) '*Ulysses*, Order and Myth', repr. in *The Modern Tradition* Ellmann & Feidelson, pp. 679–81.

Ellmann, Richard, & Feidelson, Charles T. (eds.) (1965) *The Modern Tradition* Backgrounds of modern literature. New York. Section 6: Myth.

Evans-Pritchard, E. E. (1965) *Theories of Primitive Religion* Oxford.

Farnell, L. R. (1919–20) 'The Value and Methods of Mythologic Study', *Proceedings of the British Academy*, ix, pp. 37–51.

Feder, Lillian (1971) *Ancient Myth in Modern Poetry* Princeton.

Feldman, Burton, & Richardson, Robert D. (eds.) (1972) *The Rise of Modern Mythology, 1680–1860* Bloomington. A critical anthology with invaluable bibliographies.

Ferguson, Francis (1956) '"Myth" and the Literary Scruple', *Sewanee Review*, lxiv, pp. 171–85.

Fiedler, Leslie (1952) 'Archetype and Signature: A Study of the Relationship between Biography and Poetry', *Sewanee Review*, lx, pp. 253–73.

Fontenelle, Bernard (1972) 'Of the Origin of Fables [1724]' in *The Rise of Modern Mythology, 1680–1860* Feldman & Richardson, pp. 10–18.

Fontenrose, Joseph E. (1971) *The Ritual Theory of Myth* Berkeley.

Foster, Genevieve W. (1945) 'The Archetypal Imagery of T. S. Eliot', *PMLA*, lx, pp. 567–85.

Frankfort, Henri (1958) 'Three Lectures I. The Dying God II. Heresy in a Theocratic State III. The Archetype in Analytical Psychology and the History of Religion', *Journal of the Warburg and Courtauld Institutes*, xxi, pp. 141–78.

Franklin, Howard B. (1963) *The Wake of the Gods* Melville's mythology. Stanford.

Frazer, J. G. (1911–15) *The Golden Bough* A study in magic and religion. 3rd ed. London. 12 vols.

Frazer, J. G. (ed. & trans.) (1921) *Apollodorus: the Library* London & New York. 2 vols.

Freud, Sigmund (1953–64) *Complete Psychological Works* Trans. James Strachey *et al.* London. 24 vols. [*CPW*]

Frye, Northrop (1951) 'The Archetypes of Literature', *Kenyon Review*, xiii, pp. 92–110.

Frye, Northrop (1957) *Anatomy of Criticism* Four essays. Princeton.

Frye, Northrop (Summer 1961) 'Myth, Fiction and Displacement', *Daedalus*, pp. 587–605.

Frye, Northrop (1963) *Fables of Identity* Studies in poetic mythology. New York.

Frye, Northrop (1968) 'Literature and Myth' in *Relations of Literary Study* Ed. James Thorpe. New York. pp. 27–55.

Frye, Northrop (1969) 'Mythos and Logos', *Yearbook of Comparative and General Literature* No. 18, pp. 5–18.

Fulgentius (1971) *Fulgentius the Mythographer* Trans. & intro. Leslie George Whitbread. Columbus, Ohio.

Galinsky, G. Karl (1972) *The Herakles Theme* The adaptations of the Hero in literature from Homer to the twentieth century. Oxford.

Garner, Barbara Carman (1970) 'Francis Bacon, Natalis Comes and the Mythological Tradition', *Journal of the Warburg and Courtauld Institutes*, xxxiii, pp. 264–91.

Golding, Arthur (trans.) (1961) *Shakespeare's Ovid* Being Arthur Golding's translation of the *Metamorphoses* Ed. W. H. D. Rouse. London.

Gombrich, E. H. (1945) 'Botticelli's Mythologies: a Study of the Neoplatonic Symbolism of his Circle', *Journal of the Warburg and Courtauld Institutes*, viii, pp. 7–60.

Gottfried, R. B. (1968) 'Our New Poet: Archetypal Criticism and *The Faerie Queene*', *PMLA*, lxxxiii, pp. 1362–77.

Grant, Michael (1971) *Roman Myths* London.

Graves, Robert (1951–2) 'The Language of Myth. Addenda to *The White Goddess*', *Hudson Review*, iv, pp. 5–21.

Graves, Robert (1955) *The Greek Myths* Harmondsworth. 2 vols.

Graves, Robert (1961) *The White Goddess* A historical grammar of poetic myth. London.

Greenlaw, Edwin (1932) *Studies in Spenser's Historical Allegory* Baltimore.

Gresseth, Gerald K. (1969) 'Linguistics and Myth Theory', *Western Folklore*, xxviii, pp. 153–62.

Harrison, Jane (1912) *Themis* A study of the social origins of Greek religion. With an excursus on the ritual forms preserved in Greek Tragedy by Professor Gilbert Murray and a chapter on the origin of the Olympic Games by F. M. Cornford. Cambridge.

Harrison, Jane (1913) *Ancient Art and Ritual* London.

Harrison, John S. (1924) 'Pater, Heine and the Old Gods of Greece', *PMLA*, xxxix, pp. 655–86.

Hartman, Geoffrey H. (1968) 'False Themes and Gentle Minds', *Philological Quarterly*, xlvii, pp. 55–68.

Hassan, Ihab H. (1952) 'Towards a Method in Myth', *Journal of American Folklore*, lxv, pp. 205–15.

Held, Julius S. (1961) 'Flora, Goddess and Courtesan' in *De Artibus Opuscula XL Essays in Honor of Erwin Panofsky* Ed. Millard Meiss. New York. Vol. 1, pp. 201–18.

Heninger, S. K. (1959–60) 'A Jungian Reading of "Kubla Khan"', *Journal of Aesthetics and Art Criticism*, xviii, pp. 358–67.

Herd, E. W. (1969) 'Myth Criticism: Limitations and Possibilities', *Mosaic*, ii, pp. 69–77.

Hernadi, Paul (1972) *Beyond Genre* New directions in literary classification. Ithaca & London. pp. 131–51: Northrop Frye.

Herskovits, Melville J. & Frances S. (1958) *Dahomean Narrative* A cross-cultural analysis. Evanston. pp. 81–122: A cross-cultural approach to myth.

Hoffman, Daniel (1967) *Barbarous Knowledge* Myth in the poetry of Yeats, Graves and Muir. New York.

Holloway, John (1960) 'The Concept of Myth in Literature' in *Metaphor and Symbol* Ed. L. C. Knights & Basil Cottle. London. pp. 120–32.

Holtan, Orley I. (1970) *Mythic Patterns in Ibsen's Last Plays* Minneapolis.

Hough, Graham (1966) *An Essay on Criticism* London. Ch. 20–1: Myth and archetype.

Hughes, M. Y. (1967) ' "Devils to Adore for Deities" ' in *Studies in Honour of DeWitt T. Starnes* Ed. Thomas P. Harrison *et al*. Austin. pp. 241–58.

Hungerford, Edward (1941) *Shores of Darkness* New York. pp. 62–91: Speculative mythology.

Hyman, Stanley Edgar (1949) 'Myth, Rituals and Nonsense', *Kenyon Review*, xi, pp. 455–75.

Hyman, Stanley Edgar (1958) 'The Ritual View of Myth and the Mythic' in *Myth* Sebeok, pp. 84–94.

Irwin, W. R. (1961) 'The Survival of Pan', *PMLA*, lxxvi, pp. 159–67.

Jacobi, Jolande (1959) *Complex/Archetype/Symbol in the Psychology of C. G. Jung* Trans. Ralph Manheim. London. pp. 31–73: Archetype.

Jakobson, Roman, & Lévi-Strauss, Claude (1962) ' "Les Chats" de Charles Baudelaire', *L'Homme*, ii, pp. 5–21. Trans. Katie Furness-Lane in *Structuralism* A reader. Ed. & intro. Michael Lane (1970) London. pp. 202–21.

James, E. O. (1957) 'The Nature and Function of Myth', *Folk-Lore*, lxviii, pp. 474–82.

Jung, C. G. (1953–) *Collected Works* Ed. Herbert Read, *et al*. London. 18 vols. [*CW*]

Kermode, Frank (1962) *Puzzles and Epiphanies* London. pp. 35–9: The myth kitty.

Kirk, Geoffrey S. (1970) *Myth* Its meaning and functions in ancient and other cultures. Berkeley.

Kirk, Geoffrey S. (1972) 'Aetiology, Ritual, Charter: Three Equivocal Terms in the Study of Myths', *Yale Classical Studies*, xxii, pp. 83–102.

Kissane, James (1962–3) 'Victorian Mythology', *Victorian Studies*, vi, pp. 5–28.

Kluckhohn, Clyde (1942) 'Myths and Rituals: a General Theory', *Harvard Theological Review*, xxxv, pp. 45–79.

Kocker, Robert P. (1965) 'Toward a Definition of Myth in Literature', *Thoth*, v, pp. 3–21.

Kogan, P. (1970) 'The Fascist Premises of Archetypal Criticism', *Literature and Ideology* No. 6, pp. 17–30.

Krieger, Murray (ed.) (1966) *Northrop Frye in Modern Criticism* Selected papers from the English Institute. New York.

Kuhn, Albert J. (1956) 'English Deism and the Development of Mythological Syncretism', *PMLA*, lxxi, pp. 1094–1116.

Lane, Lauriat (1954–5) 'The Literary Archetype: Some Reconsiderations', *Journal of Aesthetics and Art Criticism*, xiii, pp. 226–32.

Langbaum, Robert (1966) 'Browning and the Question of Myth', *PMLA*, lxxxi, pp. 575–84.

Law, Helen H. (1955) *Bibliography of Greek Myth in English Poetry* Folcroft.

Leach, Edmund (ed. & intro.) (1967) *The Structural Study of Myth and Totemism* London.

Leach, Edmund (1969) *Genesis as Myth* And other essays. London.

Leach, Edmund (1970) *Lévi-Strauss* London.

Lemmi, C. W. (1933) *The Classic Deities in Bacon* A study in mythological symbolism. Baltimore.

Lessa, William (1956) 'Oedipus-type Tales in Oceania', *Journal of American Folklore*, lxix, pp. 63–73.

Levin, Harry (1960) 'Some Meanings of Myth' in *Myth and Mythmaking* Murray, pp. 223–31.

Levin, Harry (1970) *The Myth of the Golden Age in the Renaissance* London.

Lévi-Strauss, Claude (1963) 'The Structural Study of Myth' in *Myth* Sebeok, pp. 50–66. Rev. & repr. in *Structural Anthropology* New York. pp. 206–31.

Lewis, C. S. (1961) *An Experiment in Criticism* Cambridge. pp. 40–9: On myth.

Lotspeich, H. G. (1932) *Classical Mythology in the Poetry of Edmund Spenser* Princeton.

Lydenberg, John (1952–3) 'Nature Myth in Faulkner's *The Bear*', *American Literature*, xxiv, pp. 62–72.

MacCaffrey, Isabel Gamble (1959) *Paradise Lost as 'Myth'* Cambridge, Mass.

Malinowski, Bronislaw (1926) *Myth in Primitive Psychology* London.

Manuel, Frank E. (1959) *The Eighteenth Century Confronts the Gods* Cambridge, Mass.

Manuel, Frank E. (1963) *Isaac Newton Historian* Cambridge, Mass. Ch. 7: The pragmatization of ancient myth.

Maranda, Pierre (ed.) (1972) *Mythology* Selected readings. Harmondsworth.

Marlow, A. N. (1961) 'Myth and Ritual in Early Greece', *John Rylands Library Bulletin*, xliii, pp. 373–402.

Martin, P. W. (1955) *Experiment in Depth* A study of the work of Jung, Eliot and Toynbee. London. Ch. 5: Archetypal images and themes.

Mauron, Charles (1963) *Des Métaphores Obsédantes au Mythe Personnel* Paris.

Merivale, Patricia (1969) *Pan the Goat-God* His myth in modern times. Cambridge, Mass.

Moorman, Charles (1956) 'Myth and Medieval Literature: *Sir Gawain and the Green Knight*', *Medieval Studies*. xviii, pp. 158–72.

Moorman, Charles (1960) *Arthurian Triptych* Mythic materials in Charles Williams, C. S. Lewis and T. S. Eliot. Berkeley.

Müller, F. Max (1880) *Lectures on the Science of Language* 6th ed. London.

Müller, F. Max (1881) 'Comparative Mythology [1856]', repr. in *Selected Essays on Language, Mythology and Religion* London. Vol. 1, pp. 299–451.

Munz, Peter (1956) 'History and Myth', *Philosophical Quarterly*, vi, pp. 1–16.

Munz, Peter (1973) *When the Golden Bough Breaks* Structuralism or Typology? London.

Murray, Henry A. (ed.) (1960) *Myth and Mythmaking* New York.

Olson, Paul A. (ed.) (1968) *The Uses of Myth* Papers relating to the Anglo-American seminar on the teaching of English at Dartmouth College, New Hampshire, 1966. Champaign, Ill.

Ong, Walter J. (1967) *In the Human Grain* Further explorations of contemporary culture. New York & London. pp. 99–126: Evolution, myth and poetic vision.

Orgel, Stephen (ed. and intro.) (1976) *The Renaissance and the Gods*. A comprehensive collection of Renaissance mythographies, iconologies, iconographies, with a selection of works from the Enlightenment. New York. 55 vols.

Ostendorf, Bernhard (1971) *Der Mythos in der Neuen Welt* Eine Untersuchung zum Amerikanischen 'Myth Criticism'. Frankfurt am Main. English abstract in *English and American Studies in German* Ed. Werner

Habicht (1972) Tübingen. pp. 178–80.

Patrides, C. A. (1965) 'The Cessation of the Oracles: the History of a Legend', *Modern Language Review*, lx, pp. 500–7.

Pike, Kenneth L. (1954) *Language in Relation to a Unified Theory of the Structure of Human Behavior* Part I. Glendale, California.

Porter, J. R. (1962) 'Samson's Riddle: Judges 14: 14, 18', *Journal of Theological Studies*, xiii, pp. 106–9.

Porter, Thomas E. (1969) *Myth and Modern American Drama* Detroit.

Prescott, Frederick Clarke (1927) *Poetry and Myth* New York.

Raglan, Fitzroy Richard Somerset (1936) *The Hero* A study in tradition, myth and drama. London.

Rahv, Philip (1953) 'The Myth and the Powerhouse', *Partisan Review*, xx, pp. 635–48.

Read, Herbert (1938) 'Myth, Dream and Poem', *transition*, xxvii, pp. 176–92.

Reinhold, Meyer (1973) *Past and Present* The continuity of classical myths. Toronto.

Riffaterre, Michael (1966) 'Describing Poetic Structures: Two Approaches to Baudelaire's "Les Chats"', *Yale French Studies*, nos. 36–7, pp. 200–42.

Righter, William (1972–3) 'Myth and Interpretation', *New Literary History*, iii, pp. 319–44.

Righter, William (1975) *Myth and Literature*. London.

Rosenfield, Claire (1968) *Paradise of Snakes* An archetypal analysis of Conrad's political novels. Chicago & London.

Rossi, Paolo (1968) *Francis Bacon* From magic to science. Trans. Sacha Rabinovitch. London. Ch. 3: The classical fable.

Sandmann, Manfred (1966) 'Percival Disguised' in *Proceedings of the IVth Congress of the International Comparative Literature Association* Ed. François Jost. The Hague & Paris. Vol. 2, pp. 897–904.

Sandys, George (1632) *Ovid's Metamorphosis* Englished, mythologized and represented in figures. Oxford. Ed. Karl K. Hulley & Stanley T. Vandersall (1970), Lincoln.

Schlegel, Friedrich (1968) 'Talk on Mythology [1800]' in *Dialogue on Poetry and Literary Aphorisms* Trans., intro. & annotated by Ernst Behler & Roman Struc. University Park & London.

Schroeter, James (1967–8) '*Redburn* and the Failure of Mythic Criticism', *American Literature*, xxxix, pp. 279–97.

Scott, Wilbur S. (ed.) (1962) *Five Approaches of Literary Criticism* New York. Section 5: The archetypal approach: literature in the light of myth.

Sebeok, Thomas A. (ed.) (1958) *Myth* A symposium. Bloomington.

Seiden, Morton Irving (1962) *William Butler Yeats* The poet as a mythmaker 1865–1939. East Lansing, Mich.

Seznec, Jean (1953) *The Survival of the Pagan Gods* The mythological tradition and its place in Renaissance humanism and art. New York.

Simonson, Harold P. (1971) *Strategies in Criticism* New York. Ch. 3: Symbolism and myth.

Slochower, Harry (1970) *Mythopoesis* Mythic patterns in the literary classics. Detroit.

Snyder, Edward (1923) *The Celtic Revival in English Literature 1760–1800* Cambridge, Mass.

Stanford, William Bedell (1954) *The Ulysses Theme* A study in the adaptability of a traditional hero. Oxford.

Starnes, DeWitt T., & Talbert, Ernest William (1955) *Classical Myth and Legend in Renaissance Dictionaries* Chapel Hill.

Stauffer, Donald A. (1948) 'The Modern Myth of the Modern Myth' in *English Institute Essays*, 1947 Ed. D. A. Robertson. New York.

Steadman, John M. (1972) 'Renaissance Dictionaries and Manuals as Instruments of Literary Scholarship: the Problem of Evidence' in *New Aspects of Lexicography*, ed. Howard D. Weinbrot. London & Amsterdam. pp. 17–35.

Symonds, John Addington (1890) *Essays Speculative and Suggestive* London. Vol. 2, pp. 126–49: Nature myths and allegories.

Thompson, Stith (1958) 'Myths and Folktales' in *Myth* Sebeok, pp. 104–10.

Tillyard, E. M. W. (1961) *Some Mythical Elements in English Literature* London.

Tindall, William York (1947) *Forces in Modern British Literature 1885–1946* New York. Ch. 9: The unconscious.

Todd, Ruthven (1946) *Tracks in the Snow* Studies in English science and art. London. pp. 29–60: William Blake and the eighteenth-century mythologists.

Trickett, Rachel (1953) 'The Augustan Pantheon: Mythology and Personification in Eighteenth-century Poetry' in *Essays and Studies 1953* London. pp. 71–86.

Trousson, Raymond (1964) *Le Thème de Prométhée dans la Littérature Européenne* Genève. 2 vols.

Tudor, Henry (1973) *Political Myth* London.

Tylor, E. B. (1873 [1871]) *Primitive Culture* Researches into the development of mythology, philosophy, religion, language, art and custom. Second ed. London. 2 vols.

Utley, Francis Lee (1960) 'Folklore, Myth and Ritual' in *Critical Approaches to Medieval Literature* Ed. Dorothy Bethurum. New York. pp. 83–109.

Vickers, Brian (1973) *Towards Greek Tragedy* Drama, myth, society. London. Part 2: Tragedy and myth.

Vickery, John B. (ed.) (1966) *Myth and Literature* Contemporary theory and practice. Lincoln.

Vickery, John B. (1972) *Robert Graves and the White Goddess* Lincoln.

Vickery, John B. (1973) *The Literary Impact of The Golden Bough* Princeton.

Vickery, John B., & J'nan, M. Sellery (eds.) (1972) *The Scapegoat* Ritual and literature. Boston.

Vico, Giambattista (1948) *The New Science* Trans. from the 3rd edition (1744) by Thomas Goddard Bergin and Max Harold Fisch. Ithaca.

Vitaliano, Dorothy B. (1973) *Legends of the Earth* Their Geologic Origins. Bloomington & London.

Vivas, Eliseo (1970) 'Myth: Some Philosophical Problems', *Southern Review*, vi, pp. 89–103.

von Abele, Rudolph (1954) '*Ulysses:* the Myth of Myth', *PMLA*, lxix, pp. 358–64.

Vries, Jan De (1967) *The Study of Religion* A historical approach. Trans. & intro. Kees W. Bolle. New York. Ch. 12: Theories concerning 'Nature Myths'.

Watt, Ian (1951) '*Robinson Crusoe* as Myth', *Essays in Criticism*, i, pp. 95–119.

Weisinger, Herbert (1964) *The Agony and the Triumph* Papers on the use and abuse of myth. East Lansing.

West, Paul (Winter 1961) '"Myth Criticism" as a Humane Discipline', *Wiseman Review*, no. 490, pp. 363–74.

Wheelwright, Philip (1968 [1954]) *The Burning Fountain* A study in the language of symbolism. New rev. ed. Bloomington.

Wheelwright, Philip (1968) 'The Archetypal Symbol' in *Perspectives in Literary Symbolism* Ed. Joseph Strelka. University Park & London. pp. 214–43.

White, John J. (1972) *Mythology in the Modern Novel* A study of prefigurative techniques. Princeton.

Willson, A. Leslie (1964) *A Mythical Image* The ideal of India in German Romanticism. Durham. pp. 93–110: The mythologists.

Wilson, E. C. (1939) *England's Eliza* Cambridge, Mass.

Wimsatt, W. K. (1966) 'Northrop Frye: Criticism as Myth' in *Northrop Frye in Modern Criticism* Krieger, pp. 75–107.

Wimsatt, W. K., & Brooks, Cleanth (1957) *Literary Criticism* A short history. New York. Ch. 31: Myth and archetype.

Zwerdling, Alex (1964) 'The Mythographers and the Romantic Revival of Greek Myth', *PMLA*, lxxix, pp. 447–56.

Index